# BBC QUIZBOOKS
# BRAIN OF SPORT

# Brain of Sport

compiled by
Chris Rhys

BBC BOOKS

Published by BBC Books
A division of BBC Enterprises Ltd
Woodlands, 80 Wood Lane, London W12 0TT

First published 1987

© British Broadcasting Corporation 1987

ISBN 0 563 20605 5

Typeset by Wilmaset, Birkenhead
Printed in Great Britain by
Richard Clay Ltd, Bungay, Suffolk

# CONTENTS

# PREFACE

*Brain of Sport* was first broadcast from the Old Cryptians Rugby club, Gloucester, in September 1975. It was then a pioneer sports programme for the BBC Radio Sports Unit, with no one certain whether the programme would be a success. Now, thirteen years on, and well over 150 programmes later, Radio 2's *Brain of Sport* is still alive and thriving in the competitive world of the sports quiz enthusiast. Much of the credit must go to the contestants, many of whom find the change from pub and club quizzes to broadcasting on national radio considerably unnerving, and it is to their credit that they overcome this hurdle, and help to produce quality programmes.

Each year some 800–1200 aspirants enter the competition, and are asked to sit an elimination round – held at Local Radio stations on the same night and at the same time. The leading 24 scorers and 6 reserves are then asked to take part in the broadcasts.

The questions for the book have been taken from the last series. Obviously it is difficult to include commentary clips and interviews from the programme in the book. Therefore some questions have been revamped to suit the style and format.

For the purpose of this book, the questions have been divided into four sections. The first section, 'Just for Openers', covers questions answered by those wishing to appear on *Brain of Sport*, and the second section, 'Brain of Sport Competition', lists the type of question given on the programme itself. To make the book more varied and enjoyable, the quizzes have been divided into eight matches, each covering a selection of sports. The matches are divided by quickfire rounds to be answered against the clock, using whatever time limit you feel just about able to beat! The third section, 'Specialist Division', lives up to its name by testing your knowledge of particular sports, with light relief provided by the 'Mixed Bag' quizzes. Finally, we challenge you to test your wits on the fourth section with the questions in 'Expert League'.

*Brain of Sport* owes a tremendous debt to Peter Jones, who has hosted every programme since the very first evening in Gloucester. This is in spite of a schedule of other Radio Sport and Outside Broadcasts which take him to Olympics, Cup Finals, Royal Ceremonies, World Cups and every major event covered by the BBC. His sympathetic handling has helped many a nervous contestant.

Thanks are also due to the series producers, Michael Tuke-Hastings (who devised the quiz), Patricia Ewing, Paul Garside, Richard Maddock, Caroline Elliot, Helen Gill and Joanne Watson, for the chores of administration, editing and guidance. Also to Ian Morrison for hours of patient verification.

The previous winners of *Brain of Sport*, those rare people with the ability to combine outstanding knowledge with the ability to think quickly and calmly under pressure, are:

1975 Patricia Arthur, Birkenhead
1976 Paul Hewitt, High Wycombe
1977 David Ball, Liverpool
1978 Julian Pincher, Telford
1979 Tony Shaw, Grimsby and St Helens
1980 Arthur Palfreyman, Matlock
1981 Derek Heys, Horwich, Bolton
1982 David Hesp, Blackpool
1983 Alex Cooke, Small Heath, Birmingham
1984 Ray Welford, Kingsley, Staffs
1985 Kerris Edwards, Sutton, Surrey
1986 Robert Tacey, Altrincham
     Graham Edge was runner up three years in succession from 1977–9.

There's an old cliché which says that records are only there to be broken. That statement is also a quiz compiler's nightmare. The questions have been checked up to and including 30 June 1987, and I am certain that readers will forgive the odd fact that may have been overtaken by events or time.

*Chris Rhys*

# 1

# JUST FOR OPENERS

# 1987 TEST QUESTIONS

70 questions to put you in the mood and get those little grey cells working!

1. Name the two beaten finalists in the 1986–7 NFL American Football League play-offs.

2. 'Pop' Robson was the first division's top scorer in 1972–3. Who was he playing for at the time?

3. In which country was former world motor racing champion Keke Rosberg born?

4. What did twenty-nine-year-old Bill Snoddy win in Edinburgh in January 1987?

5. John Williams and Doreen Wilbur, both of the United States, were, in 1972, the first post-war Olympic champions in what sport?

6. Who won Britain's two gold medals in the 1987 European indoor athletic championships?

7. Who succeeded Bjorn Borg as the men's tennis singles champion at Wimbledon?

8. The Oval staged the first test match in England. Which ground staged the second?

9. Portsmouth won the Carlsberg British Basketball League in 1986–7. Which team finished second to them, with the same number of points?

10. Who was the longest-reigning world light-heavyweight boxing champion?

11. The United Kingdom professional billiards championship was revived in 1987. Who beat Ray Edmonds in the final?

12. What did international athletes Bronislaw Malinowski, Ivo van Damme, Steve Prefontaine and Bob Gutowski have in common?

13. What is unusual about the American Bob Hope Classic golf tournament?

14. When Lloyd Honeyghan beat Johnny Bumphus at

Wembley to retain his world welterweight title in 1987, what *two* titles were at stake?

15 Name either of the two jockeys with six Epsom Derby wins to their credit; second only to Lester Piggott.

16 Who thwarted Tony McKenzie's attempts to become the fastest outright winner of a Lonsdale belt at the Fairfield Halls in January 1987?

17 Whose world championship record break of 145 did Cliff Thorburn beat in 1983?

18 Who was the second man, after Ian Botham, to score 3000 runs and take 300 wickets in test cricket?

19 Who was the 1970 Commonwealth Games middleweight boxing champion who went on to win a professional world title?

20 West Germany's Klaus-Peter Thaler won what world title in Czechoslovakia in 1987?

21 Who was the first player to make 700 Football League appearances?

22 Who partnered Eric Bristow to win the world pairs darts title at Canvey Island in February 1987?

23 What important event in horse racing history occurred on 1 May 1961?

24 Which Welshman won the Hong Kong open golf tournament on St David's Day, to become the first British winner of the title?

25 In metres, is a standard marathon: 33,185; 38,775; 40,905; 42,195; or 45,915 metres?

26 Which soccer ground staged the 1987 John Player Special final between Wigan and Warrington?

27 Who was British heavyweight boxing champion in between Joe Bugner and Gordon Ferris?

28 Who succeeded Maurice Bamford as the Great Britain Rugby League coach?

29 Which man holds the record for appearing in

thirty-three consecutive matches in the Home International soccer championship?

30 Name the hotel that staged the final of the Mercantile Credit Snooker Classic in 1987 – won by Steve Davis.

31 What does the 'S' in Frederick S. Trueman, cricketer, stand for?

32 Who was the first swimmer to complete the 100 metres breast stroke in under one minute?

33 During the war years, two Yorkshire courses staged the St Leger. York was one; name the other.

34 Name the losing boat in the 1987 America's Cup final.

35 Who is second to Jack Hobbs in the all-time list of run-makers in first class cricket?

36 Who did the British Sportswriters' Association vote as their Sportsman of the Year for 1986?

37 At which Olympics did women compete in track and field events for the first time?

38 Who hit 21 sixes in the 1986 John Player League?

39 Who was the winner of the men's singles title at the inaugural world badminton championship in 1977?

40 Martin Earley, in forty-sixth place, was the leading British Isles competitor in which famous race in 1986?

41 Who has won baseball's world series a record twenty-two times?

42 On which horse did Virginia Leng win the 1986 world three-day event championship?

43 With which sport do you associate the Boston Celtics?

44 Who won the all-Ireland Gaelic football final for the third successive year in 1986?

45 Which Dutchman won the inaugural Olympic boardsailing title in 1984?

46 Who was runner-up to Greg Norman in the 1986 British Open?

47 Whose regular girlfriend was Mines Kango?

48 Who, in 1984, was the first British gymnast to be credited with a perfect '10'?

49 Who won the third-place play-off in the 1986 world hockey championships at Willesden?

50 What is the name of the trophy presented to the winning team at the world bowls championship?

51 Pat Eddery rode Dancing Brave to victory in the 1986 King George VI and Queen Elizabeth Diamond Stakes, but who rode him to second place in the Derby?

52 In which town or city did Steve Davis win his first major professional tournament?

53 Who beat Fife Flyers 5–4 to win their first ice hockey trophy since winning the British league in 1956, thirty years earlier?

54 Name three of the four members of the Great Britain Davis Cup team beaten 4–1 by the United States in 1978.

55 Who finished bottom of the inaugural Rugby Union merit table 'A' in 1985–6?

56 What world title did Britain's Vera Menchik hold between 1927–44?

57 In which city was the final Formula One world motor racing Grand Prix of the 1986 season?

58 Who was the last Belgian to win the Tour de France?

59 Who was the next best placed British player in the European Footballer of the Year poll for 1986, after runner-up Gary Lineker?

60 Which motor racing driver piloted the Matra, March and Tyrrell cars to their first Grand Prix successes?

61 For which club side did 1986 world speedway champion Hans Nielsen ride?

62 Who won a staggering eighteen tournaments on the US golf circuit in 1945?

63 Mark Sainsbury of Australia won which world amateur title at Fistral Beach, Cornwall, in September 1986?

64 Which fellow England international lost to Eric Bristow in the final of the 1980 world professional darts championship?

65 Who was the number one ranked British male tennis player for 1986?

66 What nationality is former world dressage champion Christine Stückleberger?

67 Who was the only person to lose in *two* finals at Wimbledon in 1986?

68 What sport was re-introduced into the summer Olympic programme for the first time since 1936, in 1972?

69 In what year did Oxford begin their recent run of boat race successes which came to an end in 1986?

70 What was unusual about the 1973 international Rugby Union championship?

# 2
# BRAIN OF SPORT
# COMPETITION

# MATCH 1

## CRICKET 1

1  Which was the first first-class cricketing county to be defeated by a minor county on two occasions in the Gillette/NatWest Cup?

2  Which wicket-keeper claimed 100 victims in both 1960 and 1964?

3  Who was runner-up to Malcolm Marshall in the 1986 first-class bowling averages?

4  What record was set in 1986 by Indian test player Sandiha Aggarwahl?

5  Who took 41 wickets for Australia in the 1978–9 series against England?

6  Which 1986 first-class umpire played ice hockey and also played soccer for Grimsby Town, Hull City and Oldham Athletic?

7  Which captain won the toss in all five tests against England in 1966 and against New Zealand in 1971–2?

8  Who took 15 wickets in a test match in 1985–6?

9  Which Hampshire and England cricketer was born in Osnabrück, West Germany?

10  Which Notts cricketer scored 137 against the South Africans at Trent Bridge in 1951?

11  Who won the 1986 national village knockout title?

12  Which cricketer was the 1956 BBC Sports Personality of the Year?

# MATCH 1

## MIXED BAG 1

1 Bob Smithers was Ireland's first ever individual world champion in this sport. At the same championships Dick Clegg managed the England team to the team silver medal. Name the sport.

2 Li Lingwei of China won a world title in Jakarta in 1984. In what sport?

3 Twenty-year-old Dave Hackford, from Weymouth, was the first Briton to compete in what sport at the 1984 Olympics?

4 Which player gained 153 caps for England between 1966 and 1984 and missed just one international at Wembley during that time?

5 How many umpires are there in a game of baseball?

6 What *lift* was dropped from international weightlifting in 1972?

7 Who was John Lowe playing when he enjoyed a nine-dart finish in 1984, which netted him a cheque for £102,000?

8 Who won a swimming silver medal for Britain in the 1980 Olympic men's 200 metres butterfly final?

9 Which driver won five Grand Prix races in 1978, but finished only second to Mario Andretti in the world championship?

10 Both the 1980 British and European Formula Three champions are now current Formula One drivers. Name either.

11 Which of the following has appeared in most matches in the world snooker professional championships: John Pulman, Fred Davis or Horace Lindrum?

12 Which basketball team was bought by Manchester United?

# MATCH 1

## RUBGY LEAGUE 1

1  Who once beat Flimby and Fothergill 116–0?

2  Hull Kingston is one of the two Rugby League teams suffixed by 'Rovers'. Name the other.

3  By what name were Belle Vue Rangers originally known?

4  Which ground staged the 1982 Challenge Cup final replay between Hull and Widnes?

5  He is the youngest person to play for Great Britain and the youngest to appear in a Wembley Cup final. Name him.

6  Which was the last Rugby League team situated in the county of Lancashire?

7  Name the Wigan player who scored three tries on his Great Britain debut against France at Hull in December 1981.

8  Who kicked 16 goals in his tally of 40 points for St Helens, in their 112–0 Lancashire Cup win over Carlisle in 1986–7?

9  Who did Maurice Bamford succeed as Great Britain coach in 1984?

10  Which Hull Kingston Rovers player, in 1985–6, was the first overseas player to win the Man of Steel award?

11  Name the former New Zealand coach who took over at Wigan in 1986.

12  They have had several grounds, and names, over the years. They now play at Canal Street. Name them.

# MATCH 1

## ATHLETICS 1

1 Which German city staged the first men's Europa Cup final in 1965?

2 Whose world mile record did Roger Bannister beat in 1954?

3 Which Englishman won the silver medal in the 1974 Commonwealth Games discus, four years after winning the bronze?

4 Name either of the two men who held the UK 1500 metres record in between Brendan Foster and Steve Ovett.

5 Which English girl won the gold medal in the 100 metres at the 1978 Commonwealth Games?

6 Britain had 1–2–3 in the 800 metres at the 1986 European championship. Which other country also had a 1–2–3 in a men's track event?

7 The bronze medallist in the men's 200 metres at the 1972 Olympics later went on to win the 1980 Olympic title, and also to break the world record for the distance. Name him.

8 Who was the last American, before Dwight Stones, to hold the men's world high jump record?

9 In which town or city was Sebastian Coe born?

10 Who did Daley Thompson succeed as Olympic decathlon champion?

11 Who was the last man, before Viktor Saneyev, to successfully defend his Olympic triple jump title, back in 1964?

12 Who denied Geoff Parsons the high jump gold medal at the 1986 Commonwealth Games, by winning his second successive title?

# MATCH 1

## MOTOR CYCLING

1  Who was the fourth Japanese manufacturer to enter the competitive world of motor cycle racing?

2  Who completed the Isle of Man junior and senior TT double in both 1958 and 1959?

3  Who was the first Japanese manufacturer to provide the world 500cc champion?

4  Which Briton was denied the world 125cc title in the final round of the 1971 championship . . . his first ever world championship season?

5  Which Briton finished second to Agostini in the 1975 world 500cc championship?

6  Who dominated the 1986 world 500cc championship, winning the title from Wayne Gardner by 22 points?

7  Where was Barry Sheene involved in a spectacular crash, at 175 mph, in 1975?

8  On what make of bike did John Surtees win his world 500cc title in 1956?

9  Who was the last man to win the world 500cc championship three years in succession?

10  Which American finished third behind Barry Sheene in the 1976 and 1977 world 500cc championship?

11  In what year were the first world championships held?

12  Which fellow American finished second to Eddie Lawson in the 1984 world 500cc championship?

# MATCH 2

## SOCCER 1

1 Which of the following were *not* founder members of the football league: Nottingham Forest, Stoke City, or Derby County?

2 Who was Scotland's leading goal-scorer in the 1974 World Cup finals, with two goals?

3 Which team did Barcelona beat in the first ever Fairs Cup final?

4 Who were the first winners of the Freight Rover Trophy?

5 Tommy Docherty's unlucky thirteenth post as manager was where?

6 Who beat El Salvador 10–1 in a World Cup match in Spain in 1982?

7 Name the two teams involved in a 5–5 draw in the first division in 1984–5.

8 What notable achievement did Tony Parks manage in 1984?

9 Preston were the first winners of the Football League, but who were the first winners of the first division title?

10 Whose fifty-fifth, and final, Scottish cap was on his debut in the World Cup finals?

11 Which was the last internal English one-million-pound transfer prior to Peter Shilton in 1987?

12 Name either of the two teams involved in the first FA Cup final that drew a 100,000 crowd.

# MATCH 2

1  What is the name of the national rowing centre at Nottingham that staged the 1986 world championships?

2  How did Qamar Zaman 'beat' Jahangir Khan in the Malaysian Open final in September 1986, to register Jahangir's first 'defeat' since 1981?

3  Who rode Diester to win the 1986 British Showjumping Derby at Hickstead?

4  Who won the 1986 British professional darts championship at Redcar?

5  Who did the British Sportswriters' Association vote as their Sportswoman of the Year for 1986?

6  Which batsman scored eight centuries in the county cricket championship?

7  What national amateur championship was won by Chris Rees of Wales in August 1986?

8  In what capacity did Rene and Renato appear in Manchester in August 1986?

9  How did Fiona Macdonald make sporting history in 1986?

10  Three of the first four in the 1986 Tour de France all rode for the same team. Name it.

11  Which 1986 world champion would you associate with Wally Springett?

12  Malcolm Cooper won a gold medal with his wife at the 1986 Commonwealth Games in the small-bore rifle-shooting pairs event. What is his wife's name?

# MATCH 2

## MOTOR RACING

1 A Briton, he started in 50 Formula One Grands Prix between 1967 and 1977 without ever winning a race. Name him.

2 Who was the last non-European to win the world driver's title?

3 Which Grand Prix was included in the Formula One world championship for the one and only time in 1958?

4 Which Grand Prix was not held for twenty-seven years, following the Le Mans disaster. It then reappeared, but was held at Dijon, in France, because racing was still banned in its own country?

5 Which famous circuit returned to the Grand Prix calendar in 1985?

6 Who drove the Wolf car to its first Formula One victory in the 1977 Argentine Grand Prix, and later went on to become world champion?

7 Which motor racing circuit is situated near Tarporley in Cheshire?

8 A former champion driver, he turned to producing his own cars, but in 118 Grands Prix the car never once won. Name the driver.

9 Which American drove the Porsche, Brabham and Eagle cars to their first Formula One Grand Prix successes?

10 World champion Fangio, and runner-up Stirling Moss both drove for the same team in 1955. Name it.

11 Which race, no longer part of the Formula One driver's championship, was included between 1950 and 1960?

12 Who was the last Ferrari driver to win the world racing driver's title?

# MATCH 2

## HORSE RACING 1

1   Who was the first woman to ride a winner under Jockey Club rules?

2   Which former champion flat-race jockey was the first man to ride 1982 Grand National winner Grittar in public?

3   How many classic victories did Gordon Richards achieve as a jockey?

4   At which track, in 1947, was the first recognised night meeting in Britain?

5   Who rode Enstone Spark to victory in the 1978 One Thousand Guineas?

6   Which horse, in 1984, became the first English-trained horse to surpass career earnings of £500,000?

7   Which was the first major racing nation to adopt starting stalls?

8   Homeward Bound, in the 1964 Oaks, provided which present-day jockey with his first classic success?

9   Which famous trainer died on his seventy-fourth birthday in 1986?

10  By what name was the Derby known during the two world wars?

11  The first ever sponsored classic in England was the 1984 One Thousand Guineas. Which horse won the race?

12  Which horse did Willie Carson ride to victory in record time in the 1980 Oaks?

# MATCH 2

## CYCLING

1 Who was the best-placed British Isles rider in the 1985 Tour de France?

2 Who was the only Briton to win the famous Iron Curtain 'peace race'?

3 Which man won eight stages in the 1976 Tour de France, yet never won the race?

4 Who, in 1980, succeeded Albert Zweiffel as world professional cyclo-cross champion?

5 Tommy Simpson died on the thirteenth stage of the 1967 Tour de France. The following day, all riders let which Briton 'ride through' to take the fourteenth stage, in memoriam to Simpson?

6 Who was the last English-born rider, prior to Joey McLoughlin, to win the Tour of Britain Milk Race?

7 Who was the only Briton to win a medal at the 1984 world cycling championships at Barcelona?

8 Who broke five world records at Mexico City in January 1984?

9 On which bridge did the 1986 Milk Race finish?

10 Who has spent the last decade as world professional sprint champion?

11 Who won the 105-mile road race title at the 1986 Commonwealth Games?

12 In which country did the 1987 Tour de France start?

# QUICKFIRE ROUND 1

1   Name the ten Football League clubs that fall between Ipswich Town and Newport County . . . alphabetically speaking.

2   Name the last ten different undisputed world heavyweight boxing champions, prior to 1987.

3   Name the courses that stage the following horse races:
    1 Queen Elizabeth II Stakes
    2 Ormonde Stakes
    3 Musidora Stakes
    4 Brigadier Gerard Stakes
    5 Coventry Stakes
    6 Lockinge Stakes
    7 Princess of Wales's Stakes
    8 Waterford Crystal Mile
    9 Champagne Stakes
    10 Mill Reef Stakes

4   Name the ten leading Formula One Grand Prix drivers, reckoned in terms of career wins, as at the end of the 1986 season.

5   Name the eight counties that have won the Rugby Union county championship on three or more occasions.

# MATCH 3

## CRICKET 2

1  Who won the 1986 minor counties championship?

2  Who captained Worcestershire to their first county championship title in 1964?

3  In between Gordon Greenidge's record 163 in the John Player League and Graham Gooch's current record of 176, two men briefly held the record in 1983. Name either.

4  Who won the Man of the Match award in the 1986 Benson & Hedges Cup final?

5  Which former England keeper scored the first half-century in a Gillette Cup final?

6  Who was the last person to score a triple century in England?

7  He made the highest score in the 1986 NatWest Trophy final but did not win the Man of the Match award. Who is he?

8  Who is BBC television's test match scorer?

9  Who captained Essex to their first trophy, the 1979 Benson & Hedges Cup?

10  Which is the only current non-test playing country that took part in the second Prudential World Cup in 1979?

11  Prior to the start of the 1986 season, which England player held the record for receiving the highest sum from a benefit season (1985) – £153,906?

12  Who was the last man to take 250 wickets or more in a first-class season?

# MATCH 3

## MIXED BAG 2

1 From which city do baseball's Giants hail?

2 What do John Parrott and Joey McLoughlin have in common?

3 Name either of the two sports that take place on a piste?

4 The International Federation was formed in 1961 and the first English club was formed at Ribblesdale in 1964, with the British Federation being formed three years later. Name the sport.

5 With which sport would you associate the *non*-soccer playing Jimmy Dickinson?

6 What will Albertville be doing in 1992?

7 Which team won the county cricket championship in the same two years that Liverpool won the FA Cup for the first two times?

8 What two sports did Mike Beddow play at senior level in 1961–2?

9 Who won ten swimming world championship medals in 1973 and 1975?

10 In what year was the Le Mans tragedy, with over eighty lives being lost?

11 Which Swede won the first world rally championship in 1979?

12 Who succeeded Torvill and Dean as Britain's best ice dance pair in 1984?

# MATCH 3

## GOLF 1

1 What is the name of the competition contested by public school old boys each year?

2 Arnold Palmer won the first World Match Play final in 1964. Whom did he beat in the final?

3 Who was the last overseas player to win the US Open?

4 Which show-business personality gave his name to the first celebrity event over the Jack Nicklaus-designed St Mellion course in Cornwall in 1986?

5 Peter Thomson, and which other Australian golfer, have won the British Open since the last war?

6 He played in his only Ryder Cup in 1955, winning two matches in Great Britain's 8–4 defeat. He did, however, go on to be non-playing captain of the side in 1979 and 1981. Name him.

7 Who won his third Irish Open in 1986?

8 Which famous American golfer used a putter called 'Calamity Jane'?

9 Was the first official Ryder Cup match of 1927 held in Britain or the United States?

10 Who was the oldest winner of the US Masters, prior to Jack Nicklaus in 1986?

11 Who followed Nicklaus's 1986 Masters win by winning the US Open to prove it was 'The Year of the Geriatric'?

12 What trophy is played for at the world amateur team championship?

# MATCH 3

## RUGBY LEAGUE 2

1 Who, surprisingly, knocked Hull Kingston Rovers out of the John Player Special Trophy in 1986–7?

2 Name the Cardiff Rugby Union winger at the centre of a storm in 1986 when his identity as a Leeds Rugby League trialist was revealed.

3 Two Rugby League clubs were suspended at the start of the 1985–6 season. Southend Invicta was one. Name the other.

4 Coach Mick Blacker took which club into the Rugby League in 1984?

5 Who created a new record with a try in eleven successive first division games in 1985?

6 Who scored 55 tries in the 1984–5 season?

7 What are the christian names of New Zealand's Tamati brothers?

8 For which English team did Australian John Cogger play in 1986–7?

9 Which Doncaster player scored in every match in the 1986–7 season?

10 Who won the first Challenge Cup final to be played at Wembley?

11 Who succeeded John Woods as Leigh coach in February 1985?

12 Give the first name of the twin brother of the 1986 Lance Todd award winner.

# MATCH 3

## ATHLETICS 2

1　Who was the last Kenyan, before Julius Korir, to win the Olympic steeplechase title?

2　Originally she was called Ruth Gamm, but under what name did this athlete break several world records and win two Olympic gold medals?

3　Henri Leconte's wife was also once married to an Olympic champion – who?

4　Who was the first black captain of Britain's men's athletics team?

5　Joachim Cruz's fine win in the 800 metres at the Los Angeles Olympics broke the previous record set in 1976 – by whom?

6　Who were the brother and sister who won gold and silver medals at the 1984 Los Angeles Olympics?

7　Who were the first winners of the first division of the men's British Athletics League in 1969?

8　If you had been watching the Znamensky Memorial meeting, one of the Mobil Grand Prix series, in which city would you have been?

9　Which club did not drop a point in winning the men's first division of the British Athletics League in 1975?

10　Who broke a men's field event world record at Cork in 1984?

11　Which was the first British city, in 1934, to stage the Commonwealth Games?

12　Who was only seventeen years eight months old when he won a gold medal at the 1948 Olympics?

# MATCH 4

## SOCCER 2

1  Who was the last player to score a hat-trick in a major final at Wembley?

2  Which was the first team to win the European Cup on its *own* ground?

3  Which famous manager was appointed manager/coach of Barcelona in March 1983, and was then replaced by Terry Venables?

4  Prior to the 1986–7 season, which was the last club to score 100 League goals in a season?

5  Which club has had to apply for re-election to the League on a record fourteen occasions?

6  Which club holds the record for most points achieved in a first division season?

7  Who scored Manchester United's first goal in the 2–1 win over Liverpool in the 1977 FA Cup final?

8  Jimmy Greaves and which other player scored two goals for Spurs in their 5–1 win over Atletico Madrid in the 1963 Cup-Winners Cup final?

9  Which was the next Football League club, after Manchester United, to appear in the world club championship?

10  Who won the last European Cup final to be played in Brussels before Juventus in 1985 – eleven years earlier?

11  Jimmy Nicholson won Northern Ireland international caps with two clubs. Manchester United was one. Name the other.

12  Name either of the two teams to have won the third-division title twice since 1958–9.

# MATCH 4

## TENNIS 1

1 Who was the Briton who knocked out the fourth seed, Roscoe Tanner, in the first round of the 1977 Wimbledon championships?

2 Who has won the most men's singles matches at Wimbledon (60)?

3 Martina Navratilova and Chris Lloyd were two of the United States 1986 Federation Cup-winning team. Name the third.

4 The wife of which BBC commentator reached the semi-finals of the women's doubles at the inaugural US Open championship in 1968?

5 Roger Taylor lost three Wimbledon singles semi-finals. He was beaten by Wilhelm Bungert, Jan Kodes and who else?

6 A recent Wimbledon finalist, he was seeded number one for the Olympic demonstration tournament, yet went out early in the competition. Who was he?

7 At Wimbledon, in 1986, only one married woman did not play under her married name. Who was she?

8 What is the first name of the current top Indian player, Krishnan?

9 A British girl, she partnered Australian Wendy Turnbull in the women's doubles at the 1984 Wimbledon championship. The pair of them were seeded number two. Name the British half of the pairing.

10 He began 1985 as Britain's number one tennis player, but won only two matches in nine months. Who was he?

11 Which 1983 Wimbledon champion was, at the time, ranked no higher than 662 in the world?

12 The men's singles semi-finals at Wimbledon, in 1967, saw the rare sight of three Europeans taking part. Roger Taylor and Wilhelm Bungert were two. Name the third.

# MATCH 4

## BOXING 1

1 John H. Stracey lost his world welterweight title to Carlos Palomino in 1976. Which Briton failed in *his* attempt to beat Palomino for the title twelve months later?

2 Englishmen held the Commonwealth heavyweight title from June 1958 to July 1972, when which man ended this run of English successes?

3 What nationality is former WBC champion Alexis Arguello?

4 Against which boxer did Cassius Clay fight in his first professional bout outside the United States?

5 What is the maximum weight, in pounds, of the cruiserweight division?

6 Who was the first Ugandan-born world champion in 1979?

7 He was the first WBC cruiserweight champion and also the first IBF cruiserweight champion. Name him.

8 Floyd Patterson and Muhammad Ali were the first two men to regain the world heavyweight title. Who was the third?

9 He knocked out Mark Kaylor in 1984 and has now won a world title. Who is he?

10 Which Briton once defended his world title against Lennie Hutchins?

11 Who did Joe Bugner beat in his comeback fight in Sydney, in September 1986?

12 Which British boxer fought Marvin Hagler twice in 1978, losing both fights through cuts while holding his own?

# MATCH 4

## HORSE RACING 2

1 Who, in 1980, became the first Arab to own an English classic winner when Known Fact won the Two Thousand Guineas?

2 Lester Piggott won the last two classics of the 1984 season. Name the two races.

3 Which jockey reached 100 winners in an English season for the first time when Triple Jump won at Newmarket on 15 October 1982?

4 French trainer Criquette Head trained which horse to become the first winner of an English classic trained by a woman?

5 Who rode Secreto to victory in the Epsom Derby?

6 What is the English equivalent of the *Poule d'Essai des Pouliches*?

7 Name the odds-on favourite, beaten into second place by the winner, Petoski, in the 1985 King George VI and Queen Elizabeth Diamond Stakes.

8 Name the first English winner sired by Shergar.

9 Which horse gave Lester Piggott his last ride in the Epsom Derby?

10 On which Australian track is the Melbourne Cup run annually?

11 Name the brother and sister who, in 1984, became the first to race against each other in Britain.

12 Who trained both Santa Claus and Hard Ridden to win the Derby?

# MATCH 4

## MIXED BAG 3

1 In which sport were Scott Hamilton and Katerina Witt world champions?

2 What was the christian name of Eric Heiden's sister – winner of the overall women's world speed skating title in 1979?

3 What is the nationality of the 1986 world amateur snooker champion Paul Mifsud?

4 What relation, if any, was Horace Lindrum to Walter Lindrum?

5 Which basketball team, when assembled for the 1985–6 season, was the most expensive ever put together in the history of the British League?

6 Jack Jurek, of the United States, beat Nakeesatit Katha, of Thailand, in the final of what world championship, held at Sydney's Rushcutter Bowl in 1985?

7 Scotland staged two of this particular sport's world championships in 1984. Coatbridge held the indoor world championship, while Aberdeen staged the outdoor championship. What sport is it?

8 Karen Briggs of England retained a world title in 1984, but in which sport?

9 What event was staged for the first time at the Palais Omnisports, Bercy, Paris, in January 1985?

10 Who won the men's table tennis singles world title for Austria before the war, and for England after it?

11 In 1984, this Portuguese became world cross country champion and Olympic marathon champion. Who is he?

12 In what sport did Cambridge-born David Morgan win a gold medal for Wales at the 1986 Commonwealth Games?

# QUICKFIRE ROUND 2

1   Name the captains of the following FA Cup-winning
    teams of the 1970s:

    1970 Chelsea            1975 West Ham United
    1971 Arsenal            1976 Southampton
    1972 Leeds United       1977 Manchester United
    1973 Sunderland         1978 Ipswich Town
    1974 Liverpool          1979 Arsenal

2   Name the county cricket teams that won the Gillette
    Cup between 1964 and 1973.

    1964 .................................    1969 .................................

    1965 .................................    1970 .................................

    1966 .................................    1971 .................................

    1967 .................................    1972 .................................

    1968 .................................    1973 .................................

3   Name the nine events in which the United States won
    gold medals in the men's track and field events at the
    1984 Los Angeles Olympics.

4   Name the thirteen men who have won the world
    professional snooker championship.

5   Give the maiden names of the following ten women
    tennis stars:

    1 Judy Dalton.
    2 Margaret Du Pont.
    3 Kitty Godfree.
    4 Ann Jones
    5 Kerry Reid.
    6 Karen Susman.
    7 Margaret Court.
    8 Helen Cawley.
    9 Helen Moody.
    10 Billie Jean King.

# MATCH 5

## CRICKET 3

1 Joel Garner and Viv Richards played their last game for Somerset in a John Player League at Taunton, but against whom?

2 Who finished runners-up to Hampshire in the 1986 John Player League?

3 Which English test ground was the last to stage its first test match?

4 Which current first-class county cricket side was founded at Sidmouth, Devon, on 18 August 1875?

5 Who were the first winners of the Sheffield Shield in 1892–3?

6 Who did Bob Taylor overtake to break the world record for the number of wicket-keeping dismissals?

7 Alan Knott is England's leading wicket-keeper for test dismissals, but who is next on the list?

8 Which man, in a career stretching from 1936 to 1964, scored 123 first-class centuries?

9 The Prince of Wales is *not* the patron of one of these first-class counties. Is it Glamorgan, Gloucestershire or Surrey?

10 What does the 'T' in I. T. Botham stand for?

11 If a team batted for its allotted overs in both the NatWest and Benson & Hedges Cup finals, how many overs would it have faced in total?

12 Who captained the last England test team to play South Africa?

# MATCH 5

## AMERICAN FOOTBALL

1  Which is the only club to have won the Super Bowl two years in succession, *twice*?

2  Name either of the two teams that took part in the first American football match to be seen at Wembley, in 1983.

3  Who won the inaugural Budweiser Bowl at Crystal Palace in 1986?

4  Who scored three touchdowns in the 1985 Super Bowl?

5  To whom is the Heisman Trophy awarded each year?

6  Which was the last team to appear in consecutive Super Bowls?

7  Which was the last NFL team to change its name?

8  Who was the 1986 number one draft who turned his back on US football and went to play baseball instead?

9  Who did the Bears succeed as Super Bowl winners?

10  Who beat the Glasgow Lions 23–2 in Summerbowl II at the Alexander Stadium, Birmingham, in 1986?

11  For what trophy do the representative teams from the AFC and NFC play each January?

12  Whose home is the Anaheim Stadium?

# MATCH 5

## GOLF 2

1 The initial British Open was played over three rounds, but how many holes were there in each round?

2 Who was the first German to win the German Open?

3 The year Peter Oosterhuis finished second in the British Open, who beat him?

4 Who is the only left-hander to have won the British Open?

5 What piece of British golfing history did Mickey Walker make in November 1986?

6 Who did Greg Norman beat in a play-off, to win the 1986 European Open?

7 On which Lancashire course did Peter Thomson win the first of his five British Opens?

8 The first golfer to win £100,000 in a season on the European golf circuit achieved the feat in 1983. Who is this Briton?

9 The USA fielded two forty-two-year-olds in their 1985 Ryder Cup. Ray Floyd was one, who was the other?

10 Which European Open provided Seve Ballesteros with his first ever European tour win in 1976?

11 What does the 'D' in Arnold D. Palmer stand for?

12 What relation to each other, if any, are Gordon Brand and Gordon Brand Junior?

# MATCH 5

## RUGBY UNION

1 Eugene Cross Park is the home of which first-class Welsh club?

2 Which player left Coventry in 1983 because he was 'sick of training in the guards van of a Euston express'?

3 Whose first match, as captain of his country's team, saw a world record?

4 Which was the last of the three exiles' clubs to reach the final of the John Player Cup at Twickenham?

5 France have been beaten at home in the European championship twice in the last three home encounters by which country?

6 Which member of Ireland's 1982 Triple Crown-winning team was nicknamed 'Ginger'?

7 Which player has scored the most points in a test series for the British Lions?

8 Liverpool was the first English Rugby Union club. Which was the second?

9 The Barbarians went on their first overseas tour in 1957 – to which country?

10 Which two teams were involved in the world's highest scoring international in 1910, when 63 points were scored?

11 Who scored 18 points for the British Lions against South Africa at Cape Town in 1980?

12 He retired from international rugby in 1981 and, at that time, held the distinction of being the only man to play in four winning sides against the All Blacks. Name him.

# MATCH 5

## ATHLETICS 3

1  One of the Mobil Grand Prix series was the Nikaia meeting. In which city was it held?

2  Seb Coe's victory in the 1500 metres at the Los Angeles Olympics was a new Olympic record, erasing the record of which famous athlete?

3  Which Briton won the 1500 metres at the first three European indoor championships in 1966, 1967 and 1968?

4  Name the only Briton to win two golds at the 1986 European championships.

5  Who took Seb Coe's place in the 1500 metres after he pulled out of the 1986 Commonwealth Games?

6  Who was the first Great Britain male athlete to win an Olympic field event gold medal?

7  Who won the first ever women's Olympic marathon?

8  Who has qualified for the final of the men's 200 metres at the last four Olympics?

9  In which major 1986 Games did Canada's Ben Johnson run the second fastest 100 metres of all time?

10  Which British athlete lost his shoe during the final of the 1986 European championships 4 × 400 metres relay?

11  Yordanka Donkova headed the women's list in the 1986 Grand Prix. Who won the men's title?

12  Two British girls won European indoor titles in 1984. Name either.

# MATCH 6

## SOCCER 3

1  Which was the only Football League team playing in Europe in 1986–7?

2  Which club's record home attendance of 18,000 was set against *HMS Victory* in 1935?

3  Who did Russia beat 2–1 in the final of the first European championship in 1960?

4  What was the name of Ron Atkinson's brother who used to play alongside him in the Oxford United team in the 1960s?

5  Which club holds the record for scoring the most goals, 142, in a Scottish League season?

6  Which was the last venue, other than Hampden Park, to stage the Scottish FA Cup final ?

7  Which was the first British side to play in the European Super Cup in 1973, against Ajax?

8  Who did Phil Neal succeed as Bolton Wanderers' manager in 1985?

9  Who scored Scotland's *only* goal in the 1986 World Cup finals in Mexico?

10  With which club did former Everton star Trevor Ross begin his League career?

11  Who scored a hat-trick for Derby County against Real Madrid in the 1975–6 European Cup?

12  Who was the first manager after the war to lead a team to three first-division titles?

# MATCH 6

## HORSE RACING 3

The following questions are for the national hunt experts –

1  Which horse, in 1977, became the first to win the Mackeson and Hennessy in the same season?

2  Who was the first girl to ride a winner over fences in Britain?

3  What was the name of the 1138th, and last, winner ridden by John Francome?

4  Who was the first female jockey to ride twice in the Aintree Grand National?

5  Name the former winner of the Grand National who finished third behind ESB in Devon Loch's fateful race of 1956.

6  The national hunt jockey's title was shared in 1981–2 for the first time since 1968–9. Can you remember the names of the two jockeys who shared the honours in 1968–9?

7  Fred Winter was leading trainer every season from 1971 to 1978 except one, in 1975–6. Which trainer finished top of the list that season?

8  Who was the first trainer, in 1982–3, to saddle more than 100 national hunt winners in a season?

9  Who was the first female jockey to ride in both the Grand National and the Cheltenham Gold Cup?

10  Which horse finished second in the 1986 Grand National, at odds of 66–1?

11  Fred Winter's first Grand National success as a jockey was in 1957. On which horse?

12  Name the horse that won the 1958 Grand National by a post-war record of 30 lengths, despite carrying 6lb over weight.

# MATCH 6

## TENNIS 2

1  Which south coast British town staged the inaugural British hard court championship in 1924?

2  Although a German citizen, Bettina Bunge was not born in Germany. In which country was she born?

3  Which woman played 142 matches at Wimbledon between 1946–55, winning one singles, four doubles and five mixed-doubles titles?

4  Who was the first person to achieve the grand slam of men's doubles titles?

5  Dr Renee Richards was beaten in the first round of the 1978 US Open by reigning Wimbledon champion Virginia Wade. The last time Richards competed in a tournament was as a man. On that occasion *he* lost in the first round to the reigning 1960 Wimbledon champion. Who was that?

6  Wojtek Fibak twice won the world doubles title. One of his successful partners was Tom Okker. Name the other.

7  Who was the first male tennis player to win 100 tournaments?

8  A former Wimbledon finalist, she failed to get beyond the second round of the Olympic tennis tournament in 1984. Who is she?

9  Now an international star, she won the French and Italian junior titles in 1978 and was runner-up to Tracy Austin in that year's junior Wimbledon. Name her.

10  An international star, he won the Italian, French and Wimbledon junior titles in 1978. Name him.

11  Which county has won the men's county championship the most times?

12  What is the main court at Flushing Meadow called?

# MATCH 6

## BOXING 2

1. How many rules were in the original Queensberry Rules?

2. Under what name did Brian Harper box professionally?

3. Which famous boxer had a comeback fight against Kevin Howard whom he knocked out, but felt so out of touch with boxing that he promptly retired again?

4. At which New York venue did Floyd Patterson beat Ingemar Johansson in 1960, to regain his world heavyweight title?

5. Whom did Horace Notice replace as Commonwealth heavyweight champion?

6. Which Canadian-based British-born boxer became the first IBF super-middleweight champion in 1984?

7. Who was world heavyweight champion in between Max Schmeling and Primo Carnera?

8. What did Pete Herman do on the day of his world bantamweight title fight with Frankie Burns in 1917?

9. Who did John Conteh succeed as British light-heavyweight champion?

10. Who was the 1976 Olympic light-welterweight gold medallist who later went on to win world titles at light-middleweight and welterweight?

11. Who engaged in five world welterweight title fights, between 9–30 October 1939, and won all five?

12. Which Briton did Lee Savold beat in 1950 to claim the world heavyweight title which was only recognised by the British board?

# MATCH 6

## MIXED BAG 4

1  What is the connection between the coach of the San Diego Chargers and a West Bromwich Albion manager?

2  Who was the first sports person to appear with two different groups on *Top of the Pops* on the same night?

3  Which sport has a chain gang?

4  Bertie Hill rode Countryman III in the British gold medal-winning team at the 1956 Stockholm Olympics. Who was the owner of the horse?

5  Which world-famous sportsman, perhaps surprisingly, made his first ever visit to Ireland on 21 July 1985?

6  What did the Northern Union become in 1922?

7  Who changed their name from the Acme Packers?

8  What, in a sporting connection, was Pique?

9  Why is Bob Miller well known in 1983 sporting circles?

10  He won a scholarship from Millfield and, whilst at the school, he set a United Kingdom junior record of 22.4 seconds for the 200 yards hurdles in 1966. Name him.

11  Jimmy Daboo, a twenty-two-year-old maths student, and a Cambridge rowing cox, set an unusual record in 1984. What was it?

12  The London City Police team had to go backwards to win a gold medal for Great Britain in the 1908 Olympics – in what sport?

# QUICKFIRE ROUND 3

1. Name the ten teams that have won the first division Football League title three or more times.

2. Name the six teams that compete at cricket for Australia's Sheffield Shield, and the six that take part in the West Indian Shell Shield.

3. There are twenty Group One horse races in England. Five of them are classics. Name the other fifteen.

4. As at the start of the 1986–7 season, name England's eight most capped darts players.

5. Ten men have won seven or more professional golf 'majors'. Name them all.

# MATCH 7

## SOCCER 4

1 Who scored a first-division hat-trick on the opening day of the 1986–7 season, on his debut for his new club?

2 In which Scottish town or city is the East Stirling club based?

3 Manchester City and which other club have won the second division title a record six times?

4 Which was the last non-League club to knock a first division club out of the FA Cup?

5 Who were the brothers who went from Port Vale to Stoke City in 1982?

6 There are three Scottish League clubs based in Edinburgh: Hearts and Hibs are two. Name the third.

7 Di Stefano made international appearances for Spain, Argentina and which other country?

8 Which was the first club after the last war to win the first division title two years in succession?

9 The leading goal-scorer in the first division in the 1973–4 season played for a team that was relegated. Who is he?

10 Which Football League club was beaten 6–1 by Barnet in the FA Cup in 1976?

11 Who captained the Manchester United side that won the 1968 European Cup?

12 Which was the first Yugoslavian team to win a major European competition?

# MATCH 7

## GOLF 3

1  Which Australian holed in one during the first round of the 1983 British Open at Royal Birkdale?

2  The winner of the British Open, in addition to receiving a sizeable cheque, also receives a claret jug. However, in the first ten years of the competition what was the trophy, instead?

3  Sandy Lyle's win in the 1985 British Open was the first over par finish to win the event since 1968. Who won then?

4  Which golfer is runner-up to six-times winner Jack Nicklaus, with four victories in the US Masters?

5  Which English course staged the first Curtis Cup match in 1932?

6  An eclectic competition consists of two or more rounds. How is the scoring done?

7  Where did Britain gain that marvellous Curtis Cup victory over the Americans in 1986?

8  Which course has housed all Jersey Opens since its inception in 1978?

9  Which event gave Sandy Lyle his first US tour victory in 1986?

10  Who broke the Augusta, Georgia, course record in the 1986 US Masters?

11  Which Irishman won the 1986 Scottish Open at Haggs Castle after a play-off?

12  Which course is the home of the Lancome Trophy?

# MATCH 7

## THE OLYMPIC GAMES

1 Margaret Abbott was the first United States woman to win an Olympic gold medal. In what sport did she win that gold?

2 In what year did the Summer Games start on 27 April and finish on 31 October?

3 Who was the last woman, before Lucinda Green in 1984, to carry the flag for Britain at the opening ceremony?

4 Liechtenstein won its first ever Winter Olympics *gold* medal in 1980. Which other country, at the same Games, won its first ever medal, of any colour, in the 30 kilometres cross country?

5 An MP represented Great Britain at the 1984 Los Angeles Olympics. Name him and his constituency.

6 What was the last year that Germany competed at the Olympics as one nation?

7 Was there an Olympic celebration in 1906, yes or no?

8 Gabrielle Anderson Scheiss only finished thirty-seventh in her event at the 1984 Los Angeles Olympics, but she certainly hit the headlines. Why?

9 In what year did women first compete in the Olympics?

10 Which showjumper appeared in eight Olympics between 1948 and 1976, winning one gold, two silvers and three bronze medals?

11 Which country is identified by the official Olympic abbreviation, TCH?

12 Which was the first country to stage two Winter Olympics?

# MATCH 7

## SNOOKER

1 Which current professional once carried the Olympic torch and also boxed against Commonwealth champion Dave Sands?

2 Jimmy White won the world doubles title in 1984 when he partnered Alex Higgins. Who was his partner the previous year, when he lost 10–2 to Steve Davis and Tony Meo in the final?

3 When England first won the World Team Cup in 1981, name either of Steve Davis's two partners.

4 Who was the next member to join the Barry Hearn empire after Steve Davis, Tony Meo and Terry Griffiths?

5 Two world snooker champions both appeared in their first championship in 1979. Steve Davis was one. Name the other.

6 A current TV snooker commentator was, in his much younger days, the manager of the famous Leicester Square Hall. Name him.

7 Who, after the 1987 world championship, was second to Steve Davis in the world rankings?

8 Who won the first world professional championship to be played at the Crucible Theatre in 1977?

9 A former Southport taxi driver, and ranked sixty-ninth in the world at the time, he was a surprise finalist in the 1987 English Professional championships, where he lost to defending champion Tony Meo. Name him.

10 Which venue staged the first event of the 1986–7 season, the BCE classic?

11 Previously managed by ex-England goalkeeper Gordon Banks, he sprang a surprise by beating Cliff Thorburn in the pre-televised stages of the 1986–7 Rothmans Grand Prix. Name him.

12 Which tournament provided Steve Davis with his first major professional success in 1980?

# MATCH 7

## SPEEDWAY

1 London teams filled first and second places in the first British League in 1965: West Ham were top of the table, but which south-west London club was second?

2 Who was the first Briton, in 1981, to win the world long track championship?

3 Who was the first world long track champion in 1971 and again the following year?

4 Ole Olsen won the Midland riders championship in 1975 and 1976. He was with Coventry in 1976, but who was he with in 1975?

5 Which was David Jessup's first British League side?

6 Ole Olsen won the 1975 world championship final at Wembley. Who was the defending champion who finished second to him?

7 West Ham were the first British League winners in 1965. Who were the second winners?

8 Peter Collins and Malcolm Simmons won the world pairs title in 1977. At which English venue was the final held?

9 When David Jessup was appointed England captain in 1981, which club was he riding for?

10 With which National League team did Peter Collins start his career?

11 The first senior test series between the USA and Great Britain took place in 1980. Who captained the USA team?

12 Which team is nicknamed 'the Falcons'?

# MATCH 8

## CRICKET 4

1 Which two cricketers reached the milestone of 300 test wickets in 1984?

2 If Fred Trueman took a Hawke, what bird did Bob Willis take?

3 Who placed a £100 bet on his team to lose a John Player game?

4 Who was the first man to score a century on his test debut?

5 Who was the last man to perform the hat-trick in test cricket?

6 Who is the third, behind Sunil Gavaskar and Don Bradman, in the list of century-makers in test cricket with 26?

7 Who is the only batsman to have twice averaged more than 100 in an English season?

8 Which country has England twice dismissed for 30 runs in a test match?

9 Which will be the new minor county for 1988 to replace Somerset second XI?

10 Who has taken most catches in the history of test cricket by an outfielder?

11 A former pre-war England cricket captain, he was the first to achieve 100 catches by an outfielder in test cricket. Who was he?

12 Who captained New Zealand to their first ever victory over England, at Wellington in 1978?

# MATCH 8

## SOCCER 5

1  The 1964 Nations Cup was won by the host nation –
   who?

2  Against which club did Gordon Banks play his last
   Football League game prior to his accident?

3  The year Manchester United won the European Cup,
   another English team won a European title. Name
   them.

4  Who was the Hungarian-born player who played for
   his own national side as well as for Spain and
   Czechoslovakia?

5  Who captained Arsenal when they were beaten in the
   1952 FA Cup final by Newcastle?

6  Who captained Russia from 1954 to 1963?

7  From which club did Liverpool buy Kevin Sheedy for
   £80,000?

8  Charlton Athletic were involved in the highest-
   scoring drawn game in the Football League, when
   they drew 6–6 in 1960 – with whom?

9  Brian Clough lasted just forty-four days at Leeds
   United. Which other Leeds manager stayed for
   exactly the same length of time?

10 Which club did former Irish international Jimmy
   McIlroy manage for only eighteen days in 1970?

11 Which former Lancashire cricketer played for
   Manchester City in the 1956 FA Cup final?

12 The Scottish Football League has two 'Thistles' –
   Partick and which other?

# MATCH 8

## HORSE RACING 4

1 What, appropriately, was the name of Lester Piggott's last race as a jockey in England?

2 Dancing Brave and Shahrastani had that marvellous battle in the 1986 Epsom Derby, but which horse sneaked into third place with Steve Cauthen aboard?

3 Who trained Princess Anne's first flat-race winner, Gulfland?

4 On which horse did Lester Piggott overtake Frank Buckle's record number of classic wins?

5 Le Cantilien was third, Arcor was second, but which horse won this post-war Derby?

6 The all-time list of most wins in a career in Britain reads: Richards, Piggott, Smith, Mercer, Archer and. . . . ?

7 Who owned Diomed, the winner of the first Derby?

8 Which horse won two English classics in 1983?

9 Which jockey was placed in all five English classics in 1986?

10 Excluding 1987, name the last Epsom Derby winner whose name did *not* begin with the letter 'S'.

11 What three words were dropped from the title of the King George VI and Queen Elizabeth Stakes in 1952?

12 . . . and which (single) word was added to the title of the same race in 1975?

# MATCH 8

## TENNIS 3

1  Which country eliminated the 1985 Davis Cup runners-up, West Germany, at the first hurdle in 1986?

2  Who was the first person, male or female, to win all four grand slam events in the same year?

3  Who was seeded number twelve in the men's singles for the 1969 Wimbledon championships, when in his forty-second year?

4  Jimmy Connors's first Wimbledon singles success was in 1974. In what year was his second?

5  In which country was Ann Kiyomura born?

6  Not even ranked in the first six in his own country, he caused a major surprise by reaching the final of the 1986 French Open. Name him.

7  Who presented the Ladies' Plate to Martina Navratilova at the 1986 Wimbledon championship?

8  Including 1987, how many times has Martina Navratilova won the Wimbledon singles title as a naturalised American?

9  John McEnroe won his first tournament in almost a year, in September 1986, when he won the Volvo tournament in Los Angeles. Who did he beat in the final?

10  Who did Ivan Lendl beat 6–4, 6–2, 6–0, in the final of the 1986 US Open?

11  Give the first name of either of the two Renshaws who met each other in three Wimbledon singles finals.

12  Who was Bob Hewitt's partner when he won his first men's doubles title at Wimbledon?

# MATCH 8

## BOXING 3

1  Who did world champion Gerrie Coetzee beat for the 1971 Northern Transvaal heavyweight title?

2  Which man was manager to six world champions?

3  Which world champion was born on 30 June 1966?

4  West Ham beat Tottenham when Mark Kaylor won the British middleweight title in September 1983. Kaylor, who hailed from West Ham, defeated which man representing Tottenham?

5  From whom did Larry Holmes win the world heavyweight title?

6  Gary Cooper fought for a British boxing championship in 1985. Who outpointed him?

7  Who succeeded Larry Holmes as WBC heavyweight champion in 1984?

8  Who was the first man to stop two opponents in the first round in world heavyweight title fights?

9  Who was the first of the 1984 American Olympic champions to go on and win a professional world title?

10  What were the first names of the two men who fought for the vacant British light-welterweight title in September 1986?

11  Who was the 1974 world amateur light-heavyweight champion in Havana who went on to win the professional title four years later, yet was from an Iron Curtain country?

12  Which man did George Biddles train to become a world champion?

# QUICKFIRE ROUND 4

1   Name the ten counties that have won the county cricket championship outright on three or more occasions.

2   Name the ten heaviest boxing weights competed for at the Olympics.

3   Since their inception in 1973, only ten athletic clubs have won either the men's British League Gold Cup, or the women's Jubilee Cup. Name them.

4   Eight men have won six or more solo world motor cycling titles. Can you name them? (To help you, their nationalities and number of wins are listed below.)

| | Nationality | Wins | |
|---|---|---|---|
| 1 | Italian | 15 | .............................. |
| 2 | Spanish | 13 | .............................. |
| 3 | British | 9 | .............................. |
| 4 | Italian | 9 | .............................. |
| 5 | British | 7 | .............................. |
| 6 | British | 7 | .............................. |
| 7 | British | 6 | .............................. |
| 8 | Zimbabwean | 6 | .............................. |

5   Ten countries have staged the Summer Olympics, but *not* the Winter Games. Name them.

# 3
# SPECIALIST DIVISION

# QUIZ 1

## MIXED BAG 1

**Brigadier Gerard's Career**
1. What was Brigadier Gerard's most important win as a two-year-old?
2. The Brigadier only had one race over 1½ miles. He beat Parnell by 1½ lengths. What was the race?
3. Brigadier Gerard beat Riverman and Lord David into second and third places in his very last race, in 1972. What was it?

**Sporting Nicknames**
1. Which former world boxing champion is known as 'the Cobra'?
2. Who is known as the 'Silver Fox'?
3. 'The Walrus' is the nickname of which sportsman?

**Soccer's Golden Boot Award**
1. Who was the first winner of the European Golden Boot award in 1968?
2. Name the first British winner of the award.
3. Who was the first player, in 1970 and 1972, to win the award twice?

**All England Badminton Championships 1975-85**
1. Three Danes won the men's singles All England championship in the period 1975–85: Morten Frost and Flemming Delfs were two. Name the third.
2. Which is the only nation to have completed a men's/women's singles double in the same period?
3. Which country won their first ever men's doubles title in 1976?

# QUIZ 2

## SOCCER

**Players of the Year**

1 Who was the last overseas winner of the football writers' Player of the Year award?

2 Who was the next goalkeeper after Bert Trautmann to win the football writers' Player of the Year award?

3 Only two future England managers won the football writers' award: Don Revie was one. Name the other.

**FA Cup Captains**

1 Who captained West Brom to victory in the 1968 final against Everton?

2 Who was the last Welshman, before Everton's Kevin Ratcliffe, to captain a Cup-winning team?

3 Who proudly held aloft the Cup for Sunderland after they beat Leeds United in the 1973 final?

**Record Attendances**

1 Name either of the two clubs that attracted the biggest crowd ever, of 37,774, to a fourth division game in 1960–61.

2 Coventry were the visitors when 68,029 packed into which ground to create a second division record attendance in October 1937?

3 Maine Road and Stamford Bridge, of all the Football League grounds, have had the two largest official attendances on them. Which ground is third?

**Spanish Soccer**

1 Which was the first Spanish side, other than Real Madrid, to win one of the three major European tournaments?

2 Who has won a record twenty-three Spanish Cup finals?

3 Who finished second to Terry Venables's Barcelona in the Spanish league in 1984–5 and also won that season's Spanish Cup?

# QUIZ 3

## SNOOKER

### Rules and Equipment
1  If a player accidentally plays two reds in succession, how many points does he forfeit?
2  What is the minimum length of a cue?
3  If the black ball cannot be re-spotted on its own spot, and assuming other spots are available, where should it be re-spotted?

### Ray Reardon
1  Who did Reardon beat in the final the last time he won the world professional championship?
2  His last big win was in the 1983 Yamaha International. Who did Reardon beat 9–6 in the final?
3  Who did Reardon beat in the final the first time he won the world professional championship?

### Venues
1  A tournament, still surviving, was first held at the West Centre Hotel, Fulham, in 1975. Name it.
2  The Coral UK championship was played at Preston Guildhall every year except the first. Where was the first venue, in 1977?
3  In which city did the last world professional championship final take place before moving to Sheffield?

### World Championship Finals
1  Who was the first man since 1969 to lose two finals?
2  Two Australians have reached the final since 1969: Eddie Charlton is one. Name the other.
3  Who was the first defeated finalist, since 1969, to go on to win the title?

# QUIZ 4

## MIXED BAG 2

**What's their Sport?**
1  John Silver won a famous race in 1970 – in what sport?
2  Hans-Henrik Oersted of Denmark set five world records in Mexico City in 1979 – in what sport?
3  Mikhail Tal of Russia won a world title in 1960 – in what sport?

**Rugby League**
1  Which ground staged the first BBC floodlit competition final in 1965–6?
2  The limited-tackle rule was first seen during the 1966 competition. It was so successful that it was introduced into all matches by the end of the year. How many tackles were permitted?
3  Bramley won their first and only honour after seventy-seven years, when they won the 1973–4 BBC floodlit competition final. Who did they beat in the final?

**Ice Skating World Champions**
1  Name either of the Russians who preceded or succeeded John Curry as world champion.
2  Name the British pair that won the ice dancing title in the four years between 1966–9.
3  American girls won the women's title in 1976 and 1977. Name either of the victors.

**The 1986 Commonwealth Games**
1  Which country won both the men's and women's fours bowling competition?
2  Whose medal tally read: one gold, no silvers and no bronze medals?
3  Which was the only country, other than England or Canada, to win a boxing gold medal?

# QUIZ 5

## RUGBY UNION

**British Lions Tour Captains**
1  Why did A. E. Stoddart take over from R. L. Seddon as tour captain on the Lions' first ever tour to Australia and New Zealand?
2  Who was the first *non*-Irishman, after the last war, to be the Lions' tour captain?
3  Who was the last captain to return from a tour with an unbeaten record?

**The 1987 World Cup**
1  In which city was the final staged?
2  Which was the only country from the continent of Africa to receive an invitation?
3  Not including the 'five nations' teams and Romania, which was the only other European country represented?

**Gloucestershire's County Championships**
1  Who scored all 24 of their points when they beat Middlesex in the 1976 final?
2  Which county ended their run of three successive wins by winning the title in 1977?
3  Despite their successes, they started off the 1970s with two consecutive defeats in the final. Surrey was one county to beat them. Name the other.

**Famous All Blacks**
1  Who captained the 1967 touring All Blacks to Britain and France, leading them to victory in all four tests?
2  Who captained the All Blacks in a record thirty internationals, between 1958 and 1965?
3  Who scored a world record 26 points in an international for New Zealand against Scotland in 1982?

# QUIZ 6

## MOTOR CYCLING AND SPEEDWAY

### The Isle of Man TT Winners

1  John Surtees won the title every year from 1956–60, except 1957, when which fellow Briton won the race?
2  Who was the last man to win the senior TT and world 500cc title in the same year?
3  Which Irish rider won the race in 1976 and 1978?

### The world Pairs Speedway Championship

1  Anders Michanek of Sweden won the title in three successive years 1973–5. Who partnered him to two of those victories?
2  Who was Peter Collins's partner in the England team that won the title in 1980?
3  Bobby Schwartz and Bruce Penhall won the title for the United States in 1981. Schwartz won it again the following year, but who was his partner?

### The World Team Speedway Championship

1  Which nation prevented England from winning a third successive title by winning in 1976?
2  Which country was the first winner of the title in 1960?
3  Which was the last nation to win the title for the first time?

### Speedway Venues

1  The Brandon Stadium is the home of which team?
2  The Thornton Road Stadium was the home ground of which team until they lost their franchise in 1986?
3  Saddlebow Road is the home of which team?

# QUIZ 7

## MIXED BAG 3

**The Grand National Course**
1  Which is the highest fence on the Grand National course?
2  Beechers is fence number six on the first circuit. What is it on the second?
3  What is the fence after the Canal Turn called?

**Boxing Opponents**
1  Who was Barry McGuigan's first world title fight opponent *in* Belfast?
2  Who did Jim Watt make the last successful defence of his world lightweight title against, in Glasgow in 1980?
3  Who was Alan Minter's opponent in his first defence of his world middleweight title, in 1980?

**Referees**
1  Who was selected as Scotland's representative for the 1986 World Cup finals in Mexico?
2  He hailed from Huddersfield and was Rugby League's Referee of the Year in 1977, 1978 and 1984. Name him.
3  He refereed a Cup final in the 1930s and was a great administrator. He died recently at the age of ninety-one. Who was he?

**Darts Tournaments**
1  This event was first held in 1974 and has been won by Alan Evans, Ronnie Davies and Dave Whitcombe, amongst others. What is it?
2  Tony Skuse won it in 1981, John Lowe in 1982 and Bob Anderson in 1983. Name the tournament.
3  Leighton Rees was the first winner in 1977, Nicky Virachkul was the champion in 1979 and John Lowe in 1981. What is the event?

# QUIZ 8

## BOXING

### The Bare Knuckle Days
1 Which prize fighter was nicknamed 'the gypsy'?
2 Who is regarded as the first ever boxing champion?
3 Who drew up boxing's first set of rules in 1743?

### World Heavyweight Champions
1 Who, at 5 feet 7 inches, was the shortest world heavyweight champion?
2 Who was the last world heavyweight to weigh less than 200lb?
3 The lightest world champion since the turn of the century weighed just 181lb and reigned from 1949–51. Who was he?

### British Heavyweight World Title Contenders
1 In which city did Brian London fight Floyd Patterson for the world title in 1959?
2 In which round against Rocky Marciano did Don Cockell's world title hopes end, in 1955?
3 Who was the second Briton this century to go the distance in a world heavyweight title fight?

### First-Round Knockouts
1 He successfully defended his WBA junior-lightweight title with a first round KO over Ben Villablanca in 1983, but lost his title in the first round to Rocky Lockridge six months later. Name him.
2 Who was the last Briton to lose in the first round of a world title fight?
3 Which defending heavyweight world champion lost in the first round to Mike Dokes in 1982?

# QUIZ 9

## ATHLETICS

**Post-War British Olympic Relay Medallists**

1   A member of the silver medal-winning men's 4 × 100 metre team at the 1948 Olympics had the same surname as a member of the 4 × 100 metre bronze-winning team in 1960. Who was it?

2   Two members of the team that won the men's silver medal in the 4 × 400 metre relay in 1964 reached the individual 400 metres final. Name either.

3   Name either of the women who won medals in the sprint relay in *both* 1952 and 1956.

**Post-War British Olympic Silver Medallists**

1   Who has won Britain's only silver medal in the 5000 metres since the war?

2   Who won a silver medal behind Abebe Bikila in the marathon in 1964?

3   Britain won a silver in the women's high jump in the first four Games after the war. Name the last of the four medal winners.

**Female Sprinters**

1   Who was the Formosan girl who became the first to run 100 yards in ten seconds or less, in 1970?

2   Having equalled the world 100 metres record in 1971 and 1972, she lowered it by a tenth of a second in 1973. Name this East German girl.

3   Who was the last American girl to hold the 100 metres world record before Evelyn Ashford?

**Oldest Olympic Athletics Champions**

1   Who is Britain's oldest women's Olympic athletics champion, at thirty-three?

2   She was the oldest track champion in the women's events at the 1984 Olympics, aged thirty-four. Name her.

3   He was thirty-seven and won gold at Los Angeles in an athletics event. Who is he?

# QUIZ 10

## MIXED BAG 4

### American Sporting Venues
1 Which stadium is known as 'the house that Ruth built'?
2 Name the baseball team that plays at the Anaheim Stadium.
3 The former site of which famous American venue was once owned by the circus proprietor, Barnum?

### Freestyle Swimmers
1 Who was the first Briton to win a freestyle Olympic medal after the war?
2 Who was the last Briton to win an individual freestyle medal, prior to 1984?
3 Gordon Downie and Brian Brinkley were two members of the team that won the 4 × 200 metre freestyle bronze in 1976. Name either of the other two.

### Married Names
1 Who is Mrs Ray Washington?
2 Barry Sullivan was captain of Britain's 1972 Olympic judo team. How was his wife better known?
3 Who is the East German Mrs Meier?

### The Rules of Rugby League
1 How many points are awarded for a penalty try?
2 What is the maximum number of players allowed in the scrum?
3 What is the height of the cross bar on the goal posts?

# QUIZ 11

## GOLF

**Golf Clubs**
1 When Peter Oosterhuis won the Harry Vardon Trophy from 1972–4, which club did he represent?
2 When Sandy Lyle won the Harry Vardon Trophy on the first of two occasions, which club was he with?
3 With which club did Neil Coles spend most of his career?

**World Match Play Finals**
1 Who did Gary Player beat in the longest final – decided at the fortieth hole in 1973?
2 Seve Ballesteros's 6 and 5 win over Langer in the 1985 final was the biggest win since Gary Player beat whom 6 and 4 in the 1966 final?
3 Who did Ballesteros beat in the final the *first* time he won the title in 1981?

**Arnold Palmer**
1 Which Open provided Palmer with his first win on the US tour in 1955?
2 Palmer's last major win in Britain was in 1975 when he won what tournament at Royal St George's?
3 Palmer won the World Cup team title with two different partners: Jack Nicklaus was one. Name the other.

**British Open Venues**
1 On which course did Harry Vardon win three of his record-breaking six British Opens?
2 Which course, in 1920, staged the first Open after the First World War?
3 Archie Havers was the first winner of the Open at which course in 1923?

# QUIZ 12

## TENNIS

### Famous Doubles Pairings
1 John Newcombe won the US Open doubles title twice with different partners. Who was his partner the first time he won the title? And the second?
2 Mark Edmondson won four Australian men's doubles titles between 1980–84. Which fellow Australian partnered him to his first two successes?
3 Roy Emerson won the French men's doubles title six years in succession, 1960–65. The only non-Australian to partner him later went on to become a Wimbledon champion. Name him.

### The 1978 Davis Cup Final (USA 4:Great Britain 1)
1 Name the American doubles pairing.
2 Who did they beat 6–2, 6–2, 6–3?
3 Where was the final played?

### 1984 Olympic Tennis Championship (Exhibition)
1 Who won the men's singles?
2 Who won the women's singles?
3 Name any one of the three British youngsters who took part. (Clue: one is a Davis Cup player; two are women.)

### Rod Laver
1 When Laver won his first grand slam, in 1962, he beat Roy Emerson in three of the four finals. Whom did he beat in the other?
2 Who was the only *non*-Australian he beat in a final, when winning the grand slam in 1969?
3 The man he beat in the semi-final of the US Open and Wimbledon in 1969, later went on to win the Wimbledon title. Name him.

# QUIZ 13

## MIXED BAG 5

**Eric Bristow's World Darts Titles**
1 Who did Eric Bristow beat in his first world championship final?
2 Who did Bristow beat in the final the last time he won the world title?
3 Since he won his first title, in 1980, only three men have beaten Bristow in the world championship, Lowe is one. Name either of the other two.

**Same Name, Different Sport**
In each case there are two sports personalities, from different sports, who share the same surname which you have to try to find.
1 An international soccer-playing pair of brothers and a Commonwealth snooker player.
2 A famous squash player and former world motor racing champion.
3 A former England soccer manager and a former champion jockey on the flat.

**Russian Olympic Gymnasts**
1 She won two individual golds, was a member of the winning Russian team, and runner-up to Nadia Comanechi in the individual event in 1976. Name her.
2 Moscow hosted the 1980 Games and there was a home winner in the overall women's event. Who was the gold medallist?
3 Which man, in 1980, became the first person to win eight medals at one Olympic celebration?

**1984 Olympic Equestrian Events**
1 Which member of the British dressage team had to pull out of the competition when her horse, Dutch Courage, caught a virus?
2 Who was the American beaten in the jump-off for the individual showjumping title by Joe Fargis, a fellow countryman?
3 Which member of the British three-day event team was the first Scot to be in the team?

# QUIZ 14

## MOTOR RACING

**Niki Lauda**
1   What make of car provided Niki Lauda with his first Grand Prix success in 1974?
2   During which Grand Prix did he suffer his serious injuries in 1976?
3   Which constructor did he move to in 1978?

**French Formula One Grand Prix Drivers**
1   Prior to Alain Prost's success, the French had a poor record in the world championship. The first time a French driver finished in the first three was in 1971, when Jackie Stewart's team-mate finished third behind him. Name him.
2   When James Hunt won the world title in 1976, three Frenchmen gained points in the championship; Jacques Laffite was one. Name either of the other two.
3   Which Frenchman was James Hunt's McLaren team-mate in 1978?

**The World Constructors' Championship**
1   What was the first make of car, in 1975, 1976 and 1977, to win the title three years in succession?
2   Thanks largely to Emerson Fittipaldi winning the world title in 1974, this constructor won the Constructors' Cup. Who was it?
3   What make of car, in 1978, was the first to achieve eight Grand Prix wins in a season?

**1986 Motor Racing Championship**
1   Who was the only driver to record just one win?
2   Which was the first driver to win his own country's Grand Prix?
3   Which was Nigel Mansell's first Grand Prix victory of 1986?

# QUIZ 15

## CRICKET

**Lancashire's Gillette Cup Record**

1 After winning the Cup three years in succession, 1970, 1971 and 1972, who ended Lancashire's run of successes by defeating them in the quarter-final in 1973?
2 Clive Lloyd was Man of the Match in the 1972 final. Who was his team mate who won the award in 1970?
3 Which son of an MCC secretary captained Sussex in the 1970 final against Lancashire?

**The 1977 Centenary Test**

1 Which Middlesex opening batsman was twelfth man for England?
2 Who opened the England batting with Bob Woolmer?
3 Which Yorkshire bowler took the most wickets for England in the match?

**Young Players of the Year**

1 The last winner of the trophy to go on and play test cricket for England was the 1983 winner. Who was he?
2 Which other England captain did David Gower succeed as Young Player of the Year in 1978?
3 The 1951 Young Player of the Year was the first winner of the award to go on and captain England. Who was he?

**Badges**

1 Three *what* can be found on Middlesex's badge?
2 The Wessex Wyvern appears on which county's badge?
3 What two items can be found on Hampshire's badge?

# QUIZ 16

## MIXED BAG 6

**The 1986 World Hockey Cup**
1 Which nation, surprisingly, took the wooden spoon, finishing twelfth?
2 Who did England beat in their semi-final?
3 Which was the only country to beat England in a group match?

**Scottish Football Grounds**
Which teams play on the following home grounds:
1 Boghead.
2 Gayfield.
3 Stair Park.

**Post-War Grand Nationals**
1 Who trained the fortunate 1956 winner, ESB, to his Grand National success?
2 In the years 1964–70 inclusive, three horses sired by Vulgan won the National: Team Spirit was one. Name either of the other two.
3 Who was the last owner-trained winner of the National?

**Sportsmen's Second Names**
1 What did the 'G' in W. G. Grace stand for?
2 What does the 'W' in Jack W. Nicklaus stand for?
3 What was the great American golfer Bobby Jones's middle name?

# 4
# EXPERT LEAGUE

# EXPERT LEAGUE

## 1 SOCCER

Fifteen searching questions to test the real soccer expert –

1. Which football manager was sacked, reinstated, and sacked again within a two-month spell in 1984?

2. What did Watford Cup final captain, Wilf Rostron, have in common with the 1982 and 1983 Cup final captains?

3. Which club was forced, for the first time, in October 1986, to postpone a League game because of international call-ups?

4. Who scored the goal by which Spurs first broke the Anfield hoodoo, with a 1–0 win in March 1985, their first win over Liverpool for seventy-three years at Anfield?

5. Which former Football League club used to play its home matches at Peel Croft?

6. In which city did Pat Jennings break the British record of 109 caps?

7. Which was the last team, before West Ham in 1985–6, to score 8 goals in a first division game?

8. Crystal Palace, under Terry Venables, were to be the team of the 1980s – only it never materialised. Who took over from Venables as team manager at Palace after his departure?

9. Bobby Moore played his last game for England against Italy at Wembley in 1973. Who was his immediate successor in the number-six shirt – an equally cultured player who went on to play several games for England?

10. Who is the only goalkeeper in a major final not to concede a goal in both the match itself *and* the penalty shoot-out?

11  Which post-war League championship-winning team won the title with seven ever-presents in their team?

12  Who was the first player to be sent off during the 1986 World Cup finals?

## 2 SOCCER TRANSFER TRAIL

Which clubs did the following expensive footballers leave and join?

|   | Date | Player | Fee (£) |
|---|------|--------|---------|
| a | Aug 1980 | Kenny Sansom | 1,350,000 |
| b | Feb 1979 | Trevor Francis | 1,000,000 |
| c | Aug 1981 | Justin Fashanu | 1,000,000 |
| d | Aug 1981 | Peter Barnes | 930,000 |
| e | May 1980 | Steve Archibald | 800,000 |
| f | Jul 1979 | Mike Robinson | 756,000 |
| g | Aug 1979 | Mike Flanagan | 722,000 |
| h | Jul 1979 | Peter Barnes | 650,000 |
| i | Aug 1981 | John Chiedozie | 600,000 |
| j | Jan 1979 | David Mills | 516,000 |
| k | Aug 1979 | Asa Hartford | 500,000 |
| l | May 1980 | Peter Withe | 500,000 |
| m | Jul 1982 | Tony Woodcock | 500,000 |
| n | Aug 1966 | Alan Ball | 120,000 |
| o | Feb 1905 | Alf Common | 1,000 |

## 3 RACING CERTS

Fill in the missing winning horses of the 1980s.

| Derby | | Grand National |
|---|---|---|
| ................................ | 1980 | Ben Nevis |
| Shergar | 1981 | Aldaniti |
| Golden Fleece | 1982 | ................................ |
| Teenoso | 1983 | Corbiere |
| ................................ | 1984 | Hallo Dandy |
| Slip Anchor | 1985 | ................................ |
| Shahrastani | 1986 | West Tip |

| Cheltenham Gold Cup | | Arc de Triomphe |
|---|---|---|
| Master Smudge | 1980 | ................................ |
| ................................ | 1981 | Gold River |
| Silver Buck | 1982 | Akiyda |
| Bregawn | 1983 | ................................ |
| Burrough Hill Lad | 1984 | Sagace |
| Forgive N'Forget | 1985 | Rainbow Quest |
| ................................ | 1986 | Dancing Brave |

## 4 BRITISH BOXERS

Fill in the names of the British boxers engaged in the following world title fights.

a  1916 Flyweight
   *Winner* ..............................  *Loser* Young Zulu Kid

b  1950 Light-heavyweight
   *Winner* Joey Maxim  *Loser* ..................................

c  1953 Middleweight
   *Winner* Carl 'Bobo' Olson  *Loser* ..................................

d  1953 Flyweight
   *Winner* Yoshio Shirai  *Loser* ..................................

e  1959 Heavyweight
   *Winner* Floyd Patterson  *Loser* ..................................

f  1964 Light-heavyweight
   *Winner* Willie Pastrano  *Loser* ..................................

g  1968 Featherweight
   *Winner* Jose Legra  *Loser* ..................................

h  1971 Lightweight
   *Winner* ..............................  *Loser* Ismael Laguna

i  1976 Welterweight
   *Winner* ..............................  *Loser* Hedgemon Lewis

j  1979 Light-middleweight
   *Winner* ..............................  *Loser* Rocky Mattioli

k  1981 Junior-lightweight
   *Winner* ..............................  *Loser* Bobby Chacon

l  1983 Flyweight
   *Winner* ..............................  *Loser* Eleoncio Mercedes

m  1986 Featherweight
   *Winner* ..............................  *Loser* Danilo Cabrera

n  1986 Light-heavyweight
   *Winner* ..............................  *Loser* J. B. Williamson

## 5 THE AMERICAN CONNECTION

What do the following American teams play? (Choose from American football, baseball, basketball, soccer or ice hockey.)

| | Team | Sport |
|---|---|---|
| a | Atlanta Braves | .................................................... |
| b | Detroit Pistons | .................................................... |
| c | Houston Astros | .................................................... |
| d | Buffalo Sabres | .................................................... |
| e | Miami Dolphins | .................................................... |
| f | Calgary Flames | .................................................... |
| g | Minnesota Strikers | .................................................... |
| h | Cincinnati Bengals | .................................................... |
| i | Montreal Expos | .................................................... |
| j | Cleveland Cavaliers | .................................................... |
| k | Philadelphia 76ers | .................................................... |
| l | San Diego Sockers | .................................................... |
| m | Minnesota Vikings | .................................................... |
| n | Hartford Whalers | .................................................... |
| o | Utah Jazz | .................................................... |
| p | Kansas City Chiefs | .................................................... |
| q | San Diego Padres | .................................................... |
| r | Winnipeg Jets | .................................................... |

## 6 MIXED BAG

Twelve tricky questions to test the all-round expert –

1 Which woman won the 1978 Sullivan Award, made to the leading US amateur sports personality of the previous year?

2 Which Rugby Union club has only won half a John Player Cup?

3 On the day that St Helens RLFC scored 112 points against Carlisle in the Lancashire Cup in 1986–7, who scored 72 points against Fulham in the same competition?

4 Secreto won the 1984 Derby, but which horse was the 11–8 on favourite for the race?

5 Which boxer did Tony Sibson defeat to win a world title fight with Marvin Hagler?

6 Who is the only cyclist to have won the Tour de France before and after the last war?

7 England won the world speedway pairs title in 1976, 1977 and 1978. Which rider was a member of all three pairs?

8 Which cricketer is the common denominator of the two tied test matches?

9 Who was the cricketer who, in 1985, made a century on his debut in first class cricket – his 100 arriving in just eighty-seven minutes, out of 117 scored when he was at the crease, reaching his 100 with three consecutive sixes off Phil Carrick?

10 Which golfer was the winner of the first British Open scheduled to finish on a Sunday?

11 Who won an Olympic swimming gold medal in 1984, yet his time was slower than another competitor?

12 Bilbo Bagness won what British title for the second time in 1984?

# ANSWERS

# 1987 TEST QUESTIONS

1 Washington Redskins and Cleveland Browns.
2 West Ham United.
3 Sweden.
4 Powderhall Sprint.
5 Archery.
6 Todd Bennett and Yvonne Murray.
7 John McEnroe (1981).
8 Old Trafford.
9 Kingston.
10 Archie Moore (9 years 55 days).
11 Norman Dagley.
12 They were all killed in car crashes.
13 It is over five rounds.
14 WBC and IBF.
15 Jem Robinson or Steve Donoghue.
16 Tony Christie.
17 Doug Mountjoy.
18 Kapil Dev.
19 John Conteh.
20 Cyclo cross.
21 Jimmy Dickinson (Portsmouth, 1964).
22 Peter Locke (Wales).
23 Betting shops became legal.
24 Ian Woosnam.
25 42,195 metres.
26 Burnden Park, Bolton Wanderers FC.
27 John L. Gardner.
28 Mal Reilly (Castleford).
29 Danny Blanchflower.
30 Norbreck Castle Hotel, Blackpool.
31 Sewards.
32 Adrian Moorhouse (1987).
33 Thirsk.
34 *Kookaburra III*.
35 Frank Woolley (Kent).
36 Lloyd Honeyghan.
37 Amsterdam, 1928.
38 Ian Botham.
39 Flemming Delfs (Denmark).
40 Tour de France.

41 New York Yankees.
42 Priceless.
43 Basketball.
44 Kerry.
45 Stevan van den Berg.
46 Gordon Brand.
47 Ballyregan Bob (record-breaking greyhound).
48 Jackie McCarthy (in the vault, at Epping).
49 West Germany (beat USSR 3–2 after extra time).
50 The Leonard Trophy.
51 Greville Starkey.
52 Preston (1980 UK professional championship).
53 Nottingham Panthers.
54 David Lloyd, John Lloyd, Mark Cox, Buster Mottram.
55 Headingley.
56 Chess.
57 Adelaide.
58 Lucien van Impe (1976).
59 Ian Rush (joint sixth).
60 Jackie Stewart.
61 Oxford.
62 Byron Nelson.
63 Surfing.
64 Bobby George.
65 John Lloyd.
66 Swiss.
67 Hana Mandlikova.
68 Handball.
69 1976.
70 It was a five-way tie.

# 2 BRAIN OF SPORT COMPETITION

## MATCH 1: CRICKET 1

1 Yorkshire (by Durham, 1973, and Shropshire, 1984). 2 Bob Booth. 3 Richard Hadlee. 4 Her innings of 190 against England was a world women's test record. 5 Rodney Hogg. 6 Donald Oslear. 7 Gary Sobers. 8 Richard Hadlee (NZ) against Australia at Brisbane. 9 Paul Terry. 10 Reg Simpson. 11 Forge Valley (Yorkshire). 12 Jim Laker.

## MATCH 1: MIXED BAG 1

1 Angling. 2 Badminton. 3 Boardsailing. 4 Val Robinson (women's hockey). 5 Four (one behind the batter, and one at each of the bases 1–3). 6 The press. 7 Keith Deller. 8 Philip Hubble. 9 Carlos Reutemann. 10 Stefan Johansson (British); Michele Alboreto (European). 11 Fred Davis. 12 Warrington Vikings.

## MATCH 1: RUGBY LEAGUE 1

1 Wigan (1924–5 Challenge Cup). 2 Featherstone. 3 Broughton Rangers. 4 Elland Road (Hunslet RLFC/Leeds United AFC). 5 Shaun Edwards (Wigan). 6 Blackpool Borough. 7 Henderson Gill. 8 Paul Loughlin. 9 Frank Myler. 10 Gavin Miller. 11 Graham Lowe. 12 Runcorn Highfield.

## MATCH 1: ATHLETICS 1

1 Stuttgart. 2 Gunder Haag. 3 Bill Tancred. 4 Frank Clement or Mike Kearns. 5 Sonia Lannaman. 6 Italy (10,000 metres). 7 Pietro Mennea (Italy). 8 Pat Matzdorf (1971). 9 London (Chiswick). 10 Bruce Jenner (USA), the 1976 champion. 11 Josef Schmidt (Poland). 12 Milt Ottey (Canada).

## MATCH 1: MOTOR CYCLING

1 Kawasaki (after Honda, Suzuki and Yamaha). 2 John Surtees. 3 Yamaha. 4 Barry Sheene (Angel Nieto of Spain won the title). 5 Phil Read. 6 Eddie Lawson. 7 Daytona (he was only practising). 8 MV Augusta. 9 Kenny Roberts (1978–80). 10 Pat Hennen. 11 1949. 12 Randy Mamola.

## MATCH 2: SOCCER 1

1 Nottingham Forest (they applied and were rejected). 2 Joe Jordan. 3 London. 4 Wigan Athletic (beat Brentford in 1985). 5 Wolves. 6 Hungary. 7 QPR and Newcastle United. 8 He saved a penalty which allowed Spurs to beat Anderlecht in the 1984 EUFA Cup final. 9 Sunderland. 10 Denis Law (v Zaire, 1974). 11 Bryan Robson (October 1981). 12 Spurs and Sheffield United (at Crystal Palace, 1901).

## MATCH 2: WHAT DO YOU REMEMBER ABOUT 1986?

1 Holme Pierrepont. 2 Jahangir had to withdraw from the final through injury. 3 Paul Schockemohle (West Germany). 4 Jocky Wilson (beat Dave Whitcombe). 5 Fatima Whitbread. 6 Gordon Greenidge. 7 Welsh amateur golf championship. 8 They were the Fluminese strikers against Manchester United. 9 She became the first woman to play in the golf varsity match. 10 *La Vie Claire*. 11 Joe Johnson (he was Johnson's manager). 12 Sarah.

## MATCH 2: MOTOR RACING

1 Jackie Oliver. 2 Nelson Piquet (1983). 3 Moroccan Grand Prix. 4 Swiss Grand Prix. 5 Nurburgring. 6 Jody Scheckter. 7 Oulton Park. 8 John Surtees. 9 Dan Gurney. 10 Mercedes-Benz 11 Indianapolis 500. 12 Jody Scheckter (1977).

## MATCH 2: HORSE RACING 1

1 Meriel Tufnell. 2 Pat Eddery. 3 Fourteen.

4 Hamilton Park. 5 Ernie Johnson. 6 Time
Charter. 7 France (1963). 8 Greville Starkey. 9 Ryan
Price. 10 The *new* derby Stakes. 11 Pebbles.
12 Bireme.


## MATCH 2: CYCLING

1 Stephen Roche (third). 2 Ian Steele. 3 Freddie
Maertens (Belgium). 4 Roland Liboton (Belgium).
5 Barry Hoban (he later married Simpson's widow).
6 Matt Eaton (1983 winner – born in England but a
naturalised American). 7 Tony Doyle (5000 metres ind.
pursuit). 8 Francesco Moser (Italy). 9 Westminster
Bridge. 10 Koji Nakano (Japan). 11 Paul Curran.
12 West Germany.


# QUICKFIRE ROUND 1

1 The ten Football League clubs between Ipswich Town
and Newcastle United are:
1 Leeds United. 2 Leicester City. 3 Liverpool.
4 Luton Town. 5 Manchester City. 6 Manchester
United. 7 Mansfield Town. 8 Middlesbrough.
9 Millwall. 10 Newcastle United.

2 The last ten undisputed world heavyweight boxing
champions are:
1 Leon Spinks. 2 Muhammad Ali/Cassius Clay.
3 George Foreman. 4 Joe Frazier. 5 Sonny
Liston. 6 Floyd Patterson. 7 Ingemar Johansson.
8 Rocky Marciano. 9 Jersey Joe Walcott. 10 Ezzard
Charles.

3 The racecourses are:
1 Ascot. 2 Chester. 3 York. 4 Sandown Park.
5 Royal Ascot. 6 Newbury. 7 Newmarket.
8 Goodwood. 9 Doncaster. 10 Newbury.

4 The ten leading Formula One drivers are:
1 Jackie Stewart (27 wins). 2 Jim Clark (25
wins). 3 Niki Lauda (25 wins). 4 Alain Prost (25
wins). 5 Juan Manuel Fangio (24 wins). 6 Nelson
Piquet (17 wins). 7 Stirling Moss (16 wins). 8 Graham

Hill (14 wins). 9 Jack Brabham (14 wins). 10 Emerson Fittipaldi (14 wins).

5 The eight counties that have won the R.U. County Championship three times or more are:
1 Gloucestershire (15). 2 Lancashire (12). 3 Yorkshire (11). 4 Warwickshire (9). 5 Middlesex (8). 6 Devon (7). 7 Durham (7). 8 Kent (3).

## MATCH 3: CRICKET 2

1 Cumberland. 2 Don Kenyon. 3 Trevor Jesty (Hants – 166); Wayne Larkins (Northants – 172). 4 John Emburey (Middlesex). 5 Jim Parks (Sussex). 6 Ken Rutherford (317 for the New Zealanders against DB Close's XI at Scarborough 1986). 7 Paul Parker (Sussex – 85). 8 Wendy Wimbush. 9 Keith Fletcher. 10 Canada. 11 Graham Gooch. 12 A. P. Titch Freeman (298 in 1933).

## MATCH 3: MIXED BAG 2

1 San Francisco. 2 They both hail from Liverpool. 3 Fencing or skiing. 4 Orienteering. 5 Golf (long-time caddy for Jack Nicklaus). 6 Staging the Winter Olympics. 7 Worcestershire (1965 and 1974). 8 Cricket (for Lancashire), and Rugby League (for St Helens). 9 Kornelia Ender (East Germany). 10 1955. 11 Bjorn Waldegaard. 12 Nicky Slater and Karen Barber.

## MATCH 3: GOLF 1

1 The Halford-Hewitt Cup. 2 Neil Coles (Great Britain). 3 Greg Norman (1986). 4 Terry Wogan (won by ex-England Rugby Union captain Richard Sharp's team). 5 Kel Nagle. 6 John Jacobs. 7 Severiano Ballesteros. 8 Bobby Jones. 9 The United States (at Worcester, Massachusetts). 10 Gary Player (when he won in 1978 he was aged forty-two years, five months and nine days). 11 Ray Floyd. 12 The Eisenhower Trophy.

## MATCH 3: RUGBY LEAGUE 2

1 Doncaster. 2 Steve Ford. 3 Bridgend. 4 Mansfield
Marksmen. 5 Gary Prohm (Hull Kingston Rovers).
6 Ellery Hanley (Bradford Northern). 7 Kevin and
Howie. 8 Runcorn Highfield. 9 David Noble.
10 Wigan (beat Dewsbury 13–2). 11 Alex Murphy.
12 Kevin (brother of Bob Beardmore, Castleford).


## MATCH 3: ATHLETICS 2

1 Kip Keino (1972). 2 Ruth Fuchs (javelin). 3 Guy Drut
(1976 Olympic 100 metres hurdles champion). 4 Kriss
Akabusi. 5 Alberto Juantorena. 6 Al Joyner (gold,
triple jump) and sister Jackie (silver, heptathlon).
7 Birchfield Harriers. 8 Moscow. 9 Wolverhampton
and Bilston. 10 Yuri Sedykh (USSR), hammer.
11 London. 12 Bob Mathias (decathlon).


## MATCH 4: SOCCER 2

1 David Speedie in Chelsea's 5–4 Full Members Cup win
over Manchester City. 2 Real Madrid (1957). 3 Cesar
Luis Menotti. 4 Huddersfield Town (101 in 1979–80).
5 Hartlepool. 6 Everton (90 in 1984–5). 7 Stuart
Pearson. 8 Terry Dyson. 9 Nottingham Forest (lost to
Nacional 1–0 in 1980). 10 Bayern Munich (beat Atletico
Madrid in 1974). 11 Huddersfield Town.
12 Portsmouth or Oxford United.


## MATCH 4: TENNIS 1

1 John Lloyd. 2 Roy Emmerson. 3 Pam Shriver.
4 Gerald Williams. 5 Ken Rosewall. 6 Pat Cash.
7 Betsy Nagelsen (wife of Mark McCormack).
8 Ramesh. 9 Anne Hobbs. 10 Colin Dowdeswell.
11 Peter Fleming (McEnroe's doubles partner).
12 Nikki Pilic (Yugoslavia – the only non-European was
John Newcombe who won the title).


## MATCH 4: BOXING 1

1 Dave Green. 2 Danny McAlinden (Northern

Ireland). 3 Nicaraguan. 4 Henry Cooper (18 June 1963). 5 195lb. 6 Ayub Kalule. 7 Marvin Camel. 8 Tim Witherspoon (1986) 9 Buster Drayton (IBF light-middleweight). 10 John Conteh. 11 James Tillis. 12 Kevin Finnegan (former British and European champion).

## MATCH 4: HORSE RACING 2

1 Khalid Abdullah. 2 Oaks and St Leger. 3 Steve Cauthen. 4 Ma Biche (One Thousand Guineas). 5 Christy Roche. 6 One Thousand Guineas. 7 Oh So Sharp. 8 Maysoon. 9 Theatrical (1985). 10 Flemington Park, Melbourne. 11 Mark and Michelle Chapman (at Doncaster). 12 Mick Rogers.

## MATCH 4: MIXED BAG 3

1 Ice skating (individual champions). 2 Beth. 3 Maltese. 4 Nephew. 5 Portsmouth. 6 Ten-pin bowling. 7 Bowls. 8 Judo. 9 World indoor athletics championships. 10 Richard Bergmann. 11 Carlos Lopes (Portugal). 12 Weightlifting (82·5kg).

# QUICKFIRE ROUND 2

1 The Cup-winning captains were:
1970 Ron Harris. 1971 Frank McLintock. 1972 Billy Bremner. 1973 Bobby Kerr. 1974 Emlyn Hughes. 1975 Billy Bonds. 1976 Peter Rodrigues. 1977 Martin Buchan. 1978 Mick Mills. 1979 Pat Rice.

2 The following teams won the Gillette Cup:
1964 Sussex. 1965 Yorkshire. 1966 Warwickshire. 1967 Kent. 1968 Warwickshire. 1969 Yorkshire. 1970 Lancashire. 1971 Lancashire. 1972 Lancashire. 1973 Gloucestershire.

3 The events at which the US won gold medals at the 1984 Olympics were:
1 100 metres (C. Lewis). 2 200 metres (C. Lewis). 3 400 metres (A. Babers). 4 110 metres hurdles (R. Kingdom). 5 400 metres hurdles (E. Moses).

6  4 × 100 metres relay.  7  4 × 400 metres relay.
8  Long jump (C. Lewis).  9  Triple jump (A. Joyner).

4 The following have won the world professional snooker championship:
1 Fred Davis.  2 Joe Davis.  3 Steve Davis.  4 Walter Donaldson.  5 Terry Griffiths.  6 Alex Higgins.  7 Joe Johnson.  8 Horace Lindrum.  9 John Pulman.
10 Ray Reardon.  11 John Spencer.  12 Dennis Taylor.  13 Cliff Thorburn.

5 Their maiden names were:
1 Tegart.  2 Osborne.  3 McKane.  4 Haydon.
5 Melville.  6 Hantze.  7 Smith.  8 Gourlay.  9 Wills.
10 Moffitt.

## MATCH 5: CRICKET 3

1 Derbys.  2 Essex.  3 Bramhall Lane, Sheffield, July 1902 (Edgbaston was first used in May 1902).
4 Somerset.  5 Victoria.  6 John Murray (Middlesex).
7 Godfrey Evans.  8 Denis Compton.  9 Surrey.
10 Terence.  11 115 (60 + 55).  12 M. J. K. Smith.

## MATCH 5: AMERICAN FOOTBALL

1 Pittsburgh Steelers.  2 Minnesota Vikings; St Louis Cardinals.  3 London Ravens (beat Streatham Olympians 20-12).  4 Roger Craig (49ers).  5 The outstanding college footballer of the year.
6 Washington Redskins.  7 Indianapolis Colts.  8 Bo Jackson.  9 San Francisco 49ers.  10 Birmingham Bulls.  11 The Pro Bowl.  12 Los Angeles Rams.

## MATCH 5: GOLF 2

1 Twelve.  2 Bernhard Langer.  3 Gary Player (1974).  4 Bob Charles (1963).  5 She became the first female club professional (at Warre Club, Essex).
6 Ken Brown.  7 Royal Birkdale (1954).  8 Nick Faldo.  9 Calvin Peete.  10 Dutch open.  11 Daniel.
12 None whatsoever.

## MATCH 5: RUGBY UNION

1 Ebbw Vale. 2 Marcus Rose. (Sadly he had to leave Coventry to live in London. Now playing for Rosslyn Park.) 3 Donal Lenihan (Ireland 60; Romania 0, 1986). 4 London Welsh. 5 Soviet Union (in the FIRA championship). 6 Gerry McLoughlin. 7 Tom Kiernan. 8 Blackheath (1858). 9 Canada. 10 Wales (49); France (14). 11 Tony Ward. 12 Derek Quinnell.

## MATCH 5: ATHLETICS 3

1 Nice. 2 Kip Keino (back in 1968). 3 John Whetton. 4 Roger Black (400 metres and 4 × 400 metres relay). 5 Rob Harrison. 6 Lynn Davies (1964, long jump. Tim Ahearne, who won the triple jump in 1908, represented Ireland.) 7 Joan Benoit (USA), 1984. 8 Pietro Mennea (Italy). 9 The Goodwill Games in Moscow. 10 Brian Whittle. 11 Said Aouita (Morocco). 12 Sue Hearnshaw or Beverley Kinch.

## MATCH 6: SOCCER 3

1 Wrexham. 2 Wimbledon. 3 Yugoslavia. 4 Graham. 5 Raith Rovers (division two, 1937–8). 6 Ibrox (1924, Airdrie v Hibs). 7 Rangers – they lost 3–6 on aggregate. 8 Charlie Wright. 9 Gordon Strachan. 10 Arsenal. 11 Charlie George (including 2 penalties). 12 Matt Busby (Manchester United 1951–2, 1955–6, 1956–7).

## MATCH 6: HORSE RACING 3

1 Bachelor's Hall. 2 Jane Thorne. 3 Gratification. 4 Jenny Hembrow. 5 Royal Tan (the 1954 winner). 6 Bob Davies and Terry Biddlecombe. 7 Fred Rimell. 8 Michael Dickenson (120). 9 Linda Sheedy (National 1981; Gold Cup 1984). 10 Young Driver. 11 Sundew. 12 Mr What.

## MATCH 6: TENNIS 2

1 Torquay (it was moved to Bournemouth in

1927). 2 Switzerland. 3 Doris Hart. 4 Frank
Sedgeman. 5 Neale Fraser. 6 Karl Meiller (1976).
7 Jimmy Connors (1985). 8 Andrea Jaeger. 9 Hana
Mandlikova. 10 Ivan Lendl. 11 Middlesex. 12 The
Stadium Court.


## MATCH 6: BOXING 2

1 Twelve. 2 Brian London. 3 Sugar Ray Leonard who
came out of retirement in 1987 to win the world
welterweight title. 4 The Polo Grounds. 5 Trevor
Berbick. 6 Murray Sutherland (born Glasgow). 7 Jack
Sharkey. 8 Get married. 9 Chris Finnegan (in
1973). 10 Sugar Ray Leonard. 11 Henry Armstrong.
12 Bruce Woodcock.


## MATCH 6: MIXED BAG 4

1 They are cousins (Al and Ron Saunders). 2 Steve
Archibald (with the Spurs squad and also with the
Scotland squad, in 1982). 3 American football (they are
the crew that measure yards gained). 4 HM Queen
Elizabeth II. 5 Jack Nicklaus (he played an exhibition
against Severiano Ballesteros). 6 The Northern Rugby
League. 7 Green Bay Packers (US football team).
8 The mascot for the Mexico World Cup. 9 It is the real
name of Ben Lexcen, designer of *Australia II*'s keel in the
1983 America's Cup. 10 Gareth Edwards. 11 He was
the first man to take part in the women's boat
race. 12 Tug of war.


# QUICKFIRE ROUND 3

1 The ten teams to have won the first division title three
or more times are:
1 Liverpool (16). 2 Everton (9). 3 Arsenal (8).
4 Manchester United (7). 5 Aston Villa (7).
6 Sunderland (6). 7 Newcastle United (4). 8 Sheffield
Wednesday (4). 9 Huddersfield Town (3).
10 Wolverhampton Wanderers (3).

2 The teams competing in the Sheffield Shield are:
1 New South Wales. 2 Queensland. 3 South

Australia. 4 Western Australia. 5 Victoria.
6 Tasmania.

The teams competing in the Shell Shield are:
1 Trinidad and Tobago. 2 Leeward Islands.
3 Guyana. 4 Windward Islands. 5 Barbados.
6 Jamaica.

3 The other fifteen Group One races are:
1 Coronation Cup. 2 Ascot Gold Cup. 3 King's Stand
Stakes. 4 (Coral) Eclipse Stakes. 5 (Norcros) July
Cup. 6 King George VI and Queen Elizabeth Diamond
Stakes. 7 (Swettenham Stud) Sussex Stakes.
8 Matchmaker International (formerly Benson & Hedges
Gold Cup). 9 Yorkshire Oaks. 10 William Hill Sprint
Championship. 11 (Tattersalls) Cheveley Park
Stakes. 12 (Tattersalls) Middle Park Stakes.
13 (William Hill) Dewhurst Stakes. 14 (Dubai) Champion
Stakes. 15 (William Hill) Futurity Stakes.

4 England's eight most capped darts players are:
1 John Lowe. 2 Eric Bristow. 3 Cliff Lazarenko.
4 Bill Lennard. 5 Dave Whitcombe. 6 Alan Glazier.
7 Bobby George. 8 Tony Brown.

5 The ten golfers who have won seven or more 'majors'
are:
1 Jack Nicklaus (18). 2 Walter Hagen (11). 3 Ben
Hogan (9). 4 Gary Player (9). 5 Tom Watson
(8). 6 Harry Vardon (7). 7 Bobby Jones (7). 8 Gene
Sarazen (7). 9 Sam Snead (7). 10 Arnold Palmer (7).


## MATCH 7: SOCCER 4

1 Colin Clarke (Southampton v QPR). 2 Falkirk.
3 Leicester City. 4 Altrincham beat Birmingham 2–1 in
fourth round in 1986. 5 The Chamberlains – Mark and
Neville. 6 Meadowbank. 7 Colombia. 8 Portsmouth.
9 Mike Channon (21 goals). 10 Newport County.
11 Bobby Charlton. 12 Dynamo Zagreb (beat Leeds in
the 1967 Fairs Cup).


## MATCH 7: GOLF 3

1 Roger Davis. 2 A belt. 3 Gary Player. 4 Arnold

Palmer.  5 Wentworth.  6 A player's best score at each
hole during the entire competition is counted.
7 Kansas.  8 La Moye.  9 Greater Greensboro
Open.  10 Nick Price (63).  11 David Feherty.
12 St Nom-la-Breteche (France).


## MATCH 7: THE OLYMPIC GAMES

1 Golf (1900).  2 1908 in England.  3 Anita
Lonsbrough (1964).  4 Bulgaria (Ivan Lebanov).
5 Colin Moynihan/Lewisham East.  6 1964.  7 Yes – it
was an interim Games to mark the tenth anniversary of
the founding of the first modern Games.  8 She
staggered round the track on the final leg of the
marathon, virtually collapsing through exhaustion and
dehydration.  9 1900.  10 Raimondo D'Inzeo (Italy).
11 Czechoslovakia.  12 Switzerland (St Moritz, 1928
and 1948).


## MATCH 7: SNOOKER

1 Eddie Charlton.  2 Tony Knowles.  3 John Spencer
or David Taylor.  4 Dennis Taylor.  5 Terry Griffiths (the
1979 winner).  6 'Whispering' Ted Lowe.  7 Jimmy
White.  8 John Spencer.  9 Les Dodd.
10 Trentham Gardens, Stoke-on-Trent.  11 Joe O'Boye.
12 Coral UK professional championship (he beat Alex
Higgins in the final).


## MATCH 7: SPEEDWAY

1 Wimbledon.  2 Michael Lee.  3 Ivan Mauger.
4 Wolverhampton.  5 West Ham.  6 Anders Michanek
(Sweden).  7 Halifax.  8 Belle Vue, Manchester.
9 Kings Lynn.  10 Rochdale.  11 Scott Autrey.
12 Exeter.


## MATCH 8: CRICKET 4

1 Ian Botham and Bob Willis.  2 A crow(e) – Fred
Trueman's 300th test wicket was Neil Hawke, Bob Willis's
was Jeff Crowe.  3 Younis Ahmed – Worcs v Leics (the

game was washed out!). 4 Charlie Bannerman (165 in the very first test match in 1876–7). 5 Peter Petherick (New Zealand) 1976–7. 6 Gary Sobers. 7 Geoffrey Boycott (1971 and 1979). 8 South Africa (1895–6 Port Elizabeth; 1924 Edgbaston). 9 Wales. 10 Greg Chappell (120). 11 Wally Hammond. 12 Mark Burgess.

## MATCH 8: SOCCER 5

1 Spain. 2 Liverpool. 3 Leeds United (Fairs Cup). 4 Ladislav Kubala. 5 Joe Mercer. 6 Igor Netto. 7 Hereford United. 8 Middlesbrough. 9 Jock Stein. 10 Bolton Wanderers. 11 Jack Dyson. 12 Meadowbank Thistle.

## MATCH 8: HORSE RACING 4

1 Final Handicap (at Nottingham). 2 Mashkour. 3 Gavin Pritchard-Gordon. 4 Commanche Run (1984 St Leger). 5 Larkspur (1962). 6 Edward Hide. 7 Sir Charles Bunbury. 8 Sun Princess (Oaks and St Leger). 9 Walter Swinburn. 10 Teenoso (1983). (1986, Shahrastani; 1985, Slip Anchor; 1984, Secreto.) 11 Festival of Britain. 12 Diamond.

## MATCH 8: TENNIS 3

1 Mexico. 2 Donald Budge (1938). 3 Pancho Gonzales. 4 1982 (beat McEnroe in five sets). 5 United States. 6 Michael Penfors (Sweden). 7 Kitty Godfree. 8 Six (1982–7 inclusive). 9 Stefan Edberg (Sweden). 10 Miloslav Mecir (also of Czechoslovakia). 11 Ernest and William. 12 Fred Stolle (1962).

## MATCH 8: BOXING 3

1 Cricketer Anton Ferreira (the fight lasted 45 seconds . . . including the count). 2 Jack 'Doc' Kearns was manager of: Joey Maxim, Archie Moore, Mickey Walker, Benny Leonard, Jack Dempsey and Abe Attell). 3 Mike Tyson. 4 Roy Gumbs. 5 Ken Norton (on points in

1978). 6 Jimmy Cable. 7 Tim Witherspoon.
8 Tommy Burns (Canada). 9 Mark Breland. 10 Tony
and Clinton (they both had the same surname –
McKenzie). 11 Mate Parlov (Yugoslavia). 12 Hogan
'Kid' Bassey.

# QUICKFIRE ROUND 4

1 The ten counties that have won the cricket
championship three times or more are:
1 Yorkshire (31). 2 Surrey (18). 3 Nottinghamshire
(13). 4 Middlesex (9). 5 Lancashire (8). 6 Kent
(6). 7 Essex (4). 8 Gloucestershire (3).
9 Warwickshire (3). 10 Worcestershire (3).

2 The ten heaviest boxing weights at the Olympics are:
1 Super-heavyweight. 2 Heavyweight. 3 Light-
heavyweight. 4 Middleweight. 5 Light-middleweight.
6 Welterweight. 7 Light-welterweight. 8 Lightweight. 9 Featherweight. 10 Bantamweight.

3 The ten athletic clubs are:
1 Wolverhampton and Bilston (men; 1973, 1976–7,
1979–80). 2 Cardiff (men; 1974). 3 Edinburgh
Southern (men; 1975/women; 1975). 4 Shaftesbury
(men; 1978, 1985). 5 Haringey (men; 1981–3,
1986). 6 Birchfield Harriers (men; 1984). 7 Mitcham
(women; 1974). 8 Stretford (women; 1976–81).
9 Borough of Hounslow (women; 1982–3). 10 Essex
Ladies (women; 1984–6).

4 The eight men who have won six or more solo world
motor cycling titles are:
1 Giacomo Agostini. 2 Angel Nieto. 3 Mike
Hailwood. 4 Carlo Ubbiali. 5 Phil Read. 6 John
Surtees. 7 Geoff Duke. 8 Jim Redman.

5 The ten countries to have staged the Summer Olympics
are:
1 Greece. 2 England. 3 Sweden. 4 Belgium.
5 Holland. 6 Finland. 7 Australia. 8 Mexico.
9 Canada. 10 USSR.

# SPECIALIST DIVISION
## QUIZ 1: MIXED BAG 1

**Brigadier Gerard's Career**
1 Middle Park Stakes (it was his last race as a two-year-old). 2 King George VI and Queen Elizabeth Stakes (1972). 3 The Champion Stakes.

**Sporting Nicknames**
1 Don Curry. 2 David Taylor (snooker player). 3 Craig Stadler (golfer).

**Soccer's Golden Boot Award**
1 Eusebio (Benfica). 2 Ian Rush (1984). 3 Gerd Muller (Bayern Munich).

**All England Badminton Championships 1975-85**
1 Svend Pri (1975). 2 China (1983 and 1985).
3 Sweden (Froman and Kihlstrom).


## QUIZ 2: SOCCER

**Players of the Year**
1 Frans Thijsen (Ipswich Town, 1980–81). 2 Gordon Banks (1971–2); (Jennings won it 1972–3). 3 Joe Mercer (1949–50).

**FA Cup Captains**
1 Graham Williams. 2 Peter Rodrigues (Southampton 1976). 3 Bobby Kerr.

**Record Attendances**
1 Crystal Palace and Millwall. 2 Villa Park.
3 Goodison Park, Everton (78,299).

**Spanish Soccer**
1 Barcelona (1958 Fairs Cup). 2 Atletico Bilbao.
3 Atletico Madrid.


## QUIZ 3: SNOOKER

**Rules and Equipment**
1 Seven. 2 3 feet. 3 On the highest-value spot available.

### Ray Reardon
1 Perri Mans (1978).  2 Jimmy White.  3 John Pulman (1970).

### Venues
1 Benson & Hedges Masters.  2 Blackpool (Tower Circus).  3 Manchester (Wythenshaw Forum, 1976).

### World Championship Finals
1 Eddie Charlton (1973 and 1975 – both to Reardon).  2 Warren Simpson (1971 v John Spencer).  3 John Spencer (lost 1972, won 1977).


## QUIZ 4: MIXED BAG 2

### What's their Sport?
1 Greyhound racing (it was the name of the winning dog in the Greyhound Derby).  2 Cycling (speed records).  3 Chess.

### Rugby League
1 Knowsley Road (St Helens).  2 Four.  3 Widnes.

### Ice Skating World Champions
1 Sergei Volkov (1975); Vlademir Kovalev (1977).
2 Bernard Ford and Diane Towler.  3 Dorothy Hamill (1976); Linda Fratiane (1977).

### The 1986 Commonwealth Games
1 Wales.  2 Isle of Man (won by N. Kelly – shotgun skeet).  3 New Zealand (J. Peau – heavyweight).


## QUIZ 5: RUGBY UNION

### British Lions Tour Captains
1 Seddon drowned in Australia.  2 A. R. Smith (Scotland) to South Africa in 1962.  3 Willie John McBride (1974, to South Africa).

### The 1987 World Cup
1 Auckland (New Zealand).  2 Zimbabwe.  3 Italy.

### Gloucestershire's County Championships
1 Peter Butler.  2 Lancashire.  3 Staffordshire (1970).

### Famous All Blacks
1 Brian Lochore.  2 Wilson Whineray.  3 Alan Hewson.

## QUIZ 6: MOTOR CYCLING AND SPEEDWAY

**The Isle of Man TT Winners**
1 Bob McIntyre.  2 Giacomo Agostini (1972).  3 Tom Herron.

**The world Pairs Speedway Championship**
1 Tommy Jansson.  2 Dave Jessup.  3 Dennis Sigalos.

**The World Team Speedway Championship**
1 Australia.  2 Sweden.  3 United States.

**Speedway Venues**
1 Coventry.  2 Ellesmere Port.  3 Kings Lynn.

## QUIZ 7: MIXED BAG 3

**The Grand National Course**
1 The Chair (5ft 2in).  2 Number 22.  3 Valentines.

**Boxing Opponents**
1 Bernard Taylor (September 1986; McGuigan won in seven rounds).  2 Sean O'Grady.  3 Vito Antuofermo (the man he beat to win the title).

**Referees**
1 Brian McGinlay.  2 Billy Thompson.  3 Stanley Rous.

**Darts Tournaments**
1 The World Masters.  2 British Gold Cup.  3 World Cup (individual).

## QUIZ 8: BOXING

**The Bare Knuckle Days**
1 Jem Mace.  2 James Figg.  3 Jack Broughton.

**World Heavyweight Champions**
1 Tommy Burns (Canada).  2 Leon Spinks (196lb).
3 Ezzard Charles.

**British Heavyweight World Title Contenders**
1 Indianapolis.  2 Ninth.  3 Joe Bugner (v Ali 1975; Tommy Farr v Joe Louis was first, in 1937).

**First-Round Knockouts**
1 Roger Mayweather.  2 Pat Cowdell (to Azumah Nelson, 1985).  3 Mike Weaver.

# QUIZ 9: ATHLETICS

**Post-War British Olympic Relay Medallists**
1 Jones (Ken, 1948); (David, 1960). 2 Robbie Brightwell; Tim Graham. 3 June Paul (née Foulds); Heather Armitage.

**Post-War British Olympic Silver Medallists**
1 Gordon Pirie (1956). 2 Basil Heatley. 3 Dorothy Shirley, 1960 (the other three were Dorothy Tyler, Sheila Lerwill and Thelma Hopkins).

**Female Sprinters**
1 Chi Cheng. 2 Renate Stecher. 3 Wyomia Tyus.

**Oldest Olympic Athletics Champions**
1 Mary Peters. 2 Maricica Puica. 3 Carlos Lopes (marathon).

# QUIZ 10: MIXED BAG 4

**American Sporting Venues**
1 Yankee Stadium (named after Babe Ruth).
2 California Angels. 3 Madison Square Garden.

**Freestyle Swimmers**
1 Cathy Gibson (400 metres, 1948). 2 Bobby McGregor (100 metres, 1964). 3 Alan McClatchey; David Dunne.

**Married Names**
1 Evelyn Ashford (Olympic sprint champion and world record holder). 2 Bonnie Tyler (the singer). 3 Marita Koch (East German athlete who married her coach).

**The Rules of Rugby League**
1 Four. 2 Six. 3 10 feet (3.05 metres).

# QUIZ 11: GOLF

**Golf Clubs**
1 Pacific Harbour, Fiji. 2 Hawkstone Park. 3 Coombe Hill.

**World Match Play Finals**
1 Graham Marsh (1973). 2 Jack Nicklaus (1966).
3 Ben Crenshaw (1981).

**Arnold Palmer**
1 Canadian Open. 2 British PGA. 3 Sam Snead 1960 and 1962.

**British Open Venues**
1 Prestwick (1898, 1903, 1914). 2 Deal. 3 Troon.

## QUIZ 12: TENNIS

**Famous Doubles Pairings**
1 Roger Taylor (1971); Owen Davidson (1973). 2 Kim Warwick. 3 Manuel Santana (1963).

**The 1978 Davis Cup Final**
1 Smith and Lutz. 2 Cox and David Lloyd. 3 Palm Springs, California.

**1984 Olympic Tennis Championship (Exhibition)**
1 Stefan Edberg. 2 Steffi Graf. 3 Stuart Bale, Amanda Brown, Rina Einy.

**Rod Laver**
1 Marty Mulligan (Wimbledon). 2 Andres Gimeno (Spain), Australian championship. 3 Arthur Ashe.

## QUIZ 13: MIXED BAG 5

**Eric Bristow's World Darts Titles**
1 Bobby George (1980). 2 Dave Whitcombe (1986). 3 Keith Deller or Steve Brennan.

**Same Name, Different Sport**
1 Charlton (Bobby/Jackie and Eddie). 2 Hunt (Geoff and James). 3 Mercer (both Joe).

**Russian Olympic Gymnasts**
1 Nellie Kim. 2 Yelena Davydova. 3 Alexsandr Dityatin.

**1984 Olympic Equestrian Events**
1 Jenny Loriston-Clarke. 2 Conrad Homfeld. 3 Ian Stark.

## QUIZ 14: MOTOR RACING

**Niki Lauda**
1 Ferrari (Spanish GP). 2 German GP. 3 Brabham.

**French Formula One Grand Prix drivers**
1 François Cevert.   2 Patrick Depailler or Jean-Pierre Jarier.   3 Patrick Tambay.

**The World Constructors' Championship**
1 Ferrari.   2 McLaren.   3 Lotus.

**1986 Motor Racing Championship**
1 Gerhard Berger (Australian GP).   2 Nelson Piquet (Brazil).   3 Belgian Grand Prix.

## QUIZ 15: CRICKET

**Lancashire's Gillette Cup record**
1 Middlesex.   2 Harry Pilling.   3 M. G. Griffith.

**The 1977 Centenary Test**
1 Graham Barlow.   2 Mike Brearley.   3 Chris Old (7), 3 for 39 and 4 for 104.

**Young Players of the Year**
1 Neil Foster.   2 Ian Botham.   3 Peter May.

**Badges**
1 Seaxes.   2 Somerset.   3 (Tudor) Rose and Crown.

## QUIZ 16: MIXED BAG 6

**The 1986 World Hockey Cup**
1 India (eight times Olympic champions).   2 West Germany.   3 USSR (lost 1-0).

**Scottish Football Grounds**
1 Dumbarton.   2 Arbroath.   3 Stranraer.

**Post-War Grand Nationals**
1 Fred Rimell.   2 Foinavon (1967); Gay Trip (1970).   3 Grittar (1982 – Frank Gilman).

**Sportsmen's Second Names**
1 Gilbert.   2 William.   3 Tyre.

# EXPERT LEAGUE
## 1 SOCCER

1  John Toshack (Swansea).   2  All were suspended for the FA Cup final (Steve Foster in 1983; Glenn Roeder in 1982).  3  Shrewsbury Town.  4  Garth Crooks.
5  Burton Swifts (later Burton United). (NB Accrington used to play at Peel Park.)  6  Palma, Majorca, in 0–0 draw v Spain, 1985.  7  Southampton (beat Coventry 8–2 in 1983–4).  8  Ernie Whalley.  9  Colin Todd (Forest and Derby).  10  Helmut Ducudan (Steau Bucharest v Barcelona, 1986 European Cup final).  11  Aston Villa, 1980–1).  12  Mike Sweeney (Canada).

## 2 SOCCER TRANSFER TRAIL

a  Crystal Palace – Arsenal.  b  Birmingham City – Nottingham Forest.  c  Norwich City – Nottingham Forest.  d  West Bromwich Albion – Leeds United.
e  Aberdeen – Tottenham Hotspur.  f  Preston North End – Manchester City.  g  Charlton Athletic – Crystal Palace.  h  Manchester City – West Bromwich Albion.  i  Orient – Notts County.  j  Middlesbrough – West Bromwich Albion.  k  Nottingham Forest – Everton.  l  Newcastle United – Aston Villa.  m  FC Cologne – Arsenal.  n  Blackpool – Everton.
o  Sunderland – Middlesbrough.

## 3 RACING CERTS

*Derby*
1980   Henbit.
1984   Secreto.

*Grand National*
1982   Grittar.
1985   Last Suspect.

*Cheltenham Gold Cup*
1981   Little Owl.
1986   Dawn Run.

*Arc de Triomphe*
1980   Detroit.
1983   All Along.

## 4 BRITISH BOXERS

a Jimmy Wilde.  b Freddie Mills.  c Randolph Turpin.  d Terry Allen.  e Brian London.  f Terry Downes.  g Howard Winstone.  h Ken Buchanan. i John H. Stracey.  j Maurice Hope.  k Cornelius Boza-Edwards.  l Charlie Magri.  m Barry McGuigan. n Dennis Andries.

## 5 THE AMERICAN CONNECTION

a Baseball.  b Basketball.  c Baseball.  d Ice hockey.  e American football.  f Ice hockey. g Soccer.  h American football.  i Baseball. j Basketball.  k Basketball.  l Soccer.  m American football.  n Ice hockey.  o Basketball.  p American football.  q Baseball.  r Ice hockey.

## 6 MIXED BAG

1 Tracy Caulkins.  2 Moseley (they drew the 1982 final with Gloucester 12–12).  3 Whitehaven.  4 El Gran Senor.  5 Dwight Davison.  6 Gino Bartali (Italy). 7 Malcolm Simmons.  8 Bobby Simpson (played in the first, was Australian manager in the second).  9 Matthew Maynard (Glamorgan).  10 Tom Watson (Muirfield). 11 George di Carlo (400 metres free-time) was slower than Thomas Fahrner who won the 'B' final. 12 Orienteering.